Women in Morocco:
Participation in the Workforce
as an Avenue of Social Mobility

Rachel Alpert

The Moshe Dayan Center for Middle Eastern and African Studies seeks to contribute by research, documentation, and publication to the study and understanding of the modern history and current affairs of the Middle East and Africa. The Center is part of the School of History and the Lester and Sally Entin Faculty of Humanities at Tel Aviv University.

Women in Morocco:

Participation in the Workforce as an Avenue of Social Mobility

Rachel Alpert

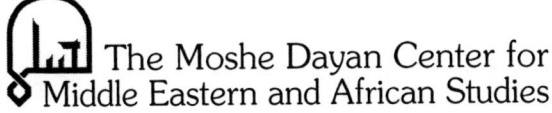 The Moshe Dayan Center for
Middle Eastern and African Studies

Tel Aviv University

Published in 2007 in Israel by
The Moshe Dayan Center for Middle Eastern and African Studies,
Tel Aviv University
Tel Aviv 69978, Israel
dayancen@post.tau.ac.il
www.dayan.org

Copyright © 2007 by Tel Aviv University

ISBN: 978-965-224-074-3

Cover design, graphic editing and production: Elena Lesnick

Printed in Israel
by Tel Aviv University Press

Table of Contents

PART IV
THE IMPACT OF WOMEN IN THE MOROCCAN WORKFORCE

Preface

The evolving status of women in Moroccan society has drawn much attention in recent years, particularly in the legal realm. Less noticed, but no less crucial, has been the accelerated entrance of Moroccan women into the workforce in recent decades. The myriad reasons for, and implications of this phenomenon are addressed by this study. By drawing upon, and synthesizing for the first time a wide range of anthropological, sociological, historical and economic sources and data, this study fills an important lacuna in the literature.

I would like to thank all of the professors at Tel Aviv University who taught me about the complexities of the Middle East and North Africa during my studies in Middle Eastern History at the Lowy School for Overseas Students. As a result, I learned a great deal about the region and its history. I would especially like to thank Dr. Bruce Maddy-Weitzman for advising me on this project, including steering me towards a number of interesting and informative sources. In addition, I am grateful to the Jack Kent Cooke Foundation for funding my studies, and to my brother Michael for reading this entire work and providing me with valuable comments and critiques.

PART I

TRADITION, COLONIALISM, AND NATIONALISM

Introduction

"Only prostitutes and insane women wandered freely in the streets," reports Fatima Mernissi in *Beyond the Veil,* as she describes the role of women in traditional Moroccan society.[1] Women were expected to remain within the confines of their house or harem walls, toiling on behalf of the family. According to the *Shari'a*, Islamic law, as well as Morocco's pre-2004 family law, it is the man's duty to provide for his wife, even if she is capable of providing for herself.[2] It is interesting to note, therefore, that between 1971 and 2002, the percentage of women in the Moroccan labor force nearly doubled from 12.6% to 24.9%.[3] What caused this increase in the percentage of women in the active workforce, running seemingly contrary to Moroccan custom and religious tradition?

In most countries, one can pinpoint an event or combination of factors as the impetus for the entrance of women into the official labor force. In the United States, World War II marked such a turning point, as the percentage of women in the workforce increased from an average of 20% between 1900 and 1930 to as high as 36% in the 1940s. The number of women in the US labor force has increased steadily since, to a current participation rate of approximately 75%.[4] In China, the communist revolution worked similarly to induce an entire generation of women to leave home in order to work for the greater good of the Communist Party. As Chairman Mao Zedong stated in the mid-1950s, "Enable every woman who can work to take her place on the labor front, under the principle of equal pay for equal work. This should be done as quickly as possible."[5] This study seeks to locate the key factors that caused a doubling of the number of Moroccan women to enter the official labor force since 1970.

While women in Morocco have always been involved in informal work around the house involving the family, this study examines the shift to the formal workforce, in which women are employed outside of their homes and earn wages for hours worked. In order to provide a comprehensive explanation for the entrance of women into the workforce, it addresses questions in five main areas:

1) **Government:** How has legislation affected and been influenced by the entrance of women into the workforce? What was the impact of government policy on the entrance of women into the labor force, and how has government

policy subsequently changed? How much of this change was driven from below and how much was driven by the king?

2) **Economy:** What roles did the international and domestic economies play in the entrance of women into the Moroccan workforce? In what ways have economic factors impacted the opportunities available to women? Why did women enter the workforce in the sectors that they did?

3) **Education:** How did educational policies affect the timing and nature of work in which women engaged? Have educational policies responded to changes in women's needs and demands as a result of their entrance into the workforce?

4) **Religion:** How did religion impact the entrance of women into the workforce? How did the religious establishment respond to the societal changes that ensued when women began to work?

5) **Norms:** What impact did the entrance of women into the workforce have on family life in terms of spousal relations, familial hierarchy, marriage age, and family planning? Has the status of women changed as a result of their increasing rates of participation in the workforce? Does the impact that this had on women's status differ between the public and familial realms?

In order to tackle these issues, this study is divided into four parts. Part I looks at the situation prior to the entrance of women into the Moroccan workforce, setting the stage for their entrance. It covers pre-colonial societal norms and the role of women in Moroccan society, the colonial period, and its aftermath. Part II focuses on the plethora of forces that coincided to induce women to enter the workforce in significant numbers beginning in the 1970s. These forces include education, the economy, laws, and social movements. Part III examines what kind of work women did and why. Part IV attempts to explain the impact of the entrance of Moroccan women into the official, wage-earning workforce on the above-mentioned factors – society, law, family life, and family planning.

This paper concludes that women entered the Moroccan workforce for a variety of reasons. Wealthier urban women started to work because they had received an education, and their families supported their endeavors. Rural or lower class women began working out of necessity as economic changes of the late 1970s and increased rural to urban migration forced many women to work to make ends meet. Urban migration also provided women with previously unavailable opportunities to work outside the house in such areas as manufacturing and domestic service. In addition, exposure to international markets and globalization influenced the type of work available and the attitudes of Moroccan rulers towards women in the workforce.

While societal views have slowly shifted along with these changes, many cultural and religious norms regarding women and work remain extant. A woman's entrance into the workforce is a common source of marital strain, as a husband may regard his wife's presence in the public sphere as an affront to his honor. Such religious and cultural considerations impact the type of work that women undertake as well as the number of women that are educated and can find work. Regardless of familial and religious pressures, however, the number of women in the Moroccan workforce increased dramatically during the last three decades of the twentieth century and into the new millennium.

The increase in working women during these years affected societal norms and family planning as the idea of women engaging in the workforce outside of the house grew less foreign. While many women preferred not to work, many could not find jobs, and many were looked down upon for trying, societal norms slowly shifted, enabling more women than before to work outside of the home for their own salaries, thus making women increasingly active members of Moroccan society. This ultimately laid the foundation for legal and social change, highlighted by the adoption in 2004 of a new and sharply altered Family Code.

The Scope of Relevant Literature

While there are no comprehensive studies on the entrance of women into the Moroccan workforce, a number of people have written about women in Morocco, hailing from a variety of disciplines: Anthropology, Sociology, Economics, Political Science, and History.

Many books have discussed facets of the complex picture that caused women to begin to work in greater numbers. Fatima Agnaou analyzes Moroccan literacy campaigns in *Gender, Literacy, and Empowerment in Morocco*. Susan S. Davis lived in a Moroccan village from 1970 to 1972 and wrote about the role of women there in *Patience and Power: Women's Lives in a Moroccan Village*. Vanessa Maher studied and interviewed women in Morocco in the early 1970s in *Women and Property in Morocco: Their Changing Relation to the Process of Social Stratification in the Middle Atlas*. Margaret Rausch, in *Bodies, Boundaries and Spirit Possession: Moroccan Women and the Revision of Tradition*, looks at Moroccan women who work as female seers (*shuwwafat*). The book's discussion of changing societal norms and its compilations of interviews with Moroccan women are particularly useful. Deborah Kapchan also discusses shifts in societal norms in *Gender on the Market: Moroccan Women and the Revoicing of Tradition*, in which she relays the changing nature of female participation in rural Moroccan markets.

For information on legal matters, Julie Combe's *La Condition de la Femme Marocaine* discusses Morocco in the international legal context, while Ziba Mir-Hosseini looks at domestic family law in *Marriage on Trial: A Study of Islamic Family Law*. She carried out her research by observing the courts of Morocco for a year, interviewing judges, reading cases, and speaking with participants in legal proceedings. In addition, Zakya Daoud's *Feminisme et Politique au Maghreb* details legal changes and political movements affecting women throughout the twentieth century.

Economic data about Morocco in this time period abounds. I. William Zartman edited an important volume on this topic: *The Political Economy of Morocco*. In addition, Guilain P. Denoeux and Abdeslam Maghraoui wrote about the economic climate of Morocco between 1983 and 1990 in their chapter, "The Political Economy of Structural Adjustment in Morocco," in Layachi (ed.), *Economic Crisis and Political Change in North Africa*. Through such works as *Women, Work and Economic Reform in the Middle East and North Africa* and "Enhancing Women's Economic Participation in the MENA Region," in Handousa and Tzannatos (eds.), *Employment Creation and Social Protection in the Middle East and North Africa*, Valentine M. Moghadam looks specifically at the relationship between economic changes in North Africa and women in the labor force. There are also a number of statistical databases that detail labor trends and employment numbers in Morocco, including those of the World Bank and the International Labor Organization.

For analyses of family planning, Youssef Courbage's "Demographic Change in the Arab World: The Impact of Migration, Education and Taxes in Egypt and Morocco," Claire Griffiths's "Social Development and Women in Africa: The Case of Morocco," Bruce Maddy-Weitzman's "Population Growth and Family Planning in Morocco," and Georges Sabagh's "The Challenges of Population Growth in Morocco," provide useful information and data on trends and societal factors.

Finally, Fatima Mernissi's books provide an unparalleled window into what life is like as a woman in Morocco. Mernissi is a modern Moroccan woman who uses her experiences and training as a sociologist to write insightful books about gender relations in Morocco. *Beyond the Veil*, for example, paints a nuanced and convincing description of gender relations and women's roles in Moroccan society. It explains and interprets the religious basis and traditional reasons for societal segregation of men and women, yet also notes changes over the course of the 20th century that lay the groundwork for the entrance of women into the workforce.

This study complements the existing literature by reaching across disciplines to coalesce the contributions of anthropological, economic, political science, sociological, and historical sources, to create a comprehensive picture of why women entered the workforce in Morocco and what impact this had on Moroccan society and the economy. Anthropological and sociological studies paint a picture of the social situation that women faced upon their entrance into the workforce. Available economic data provides another dimension to this anthropological data, allowing the description of both the individual, humanistic side to the story, while also looking at the overall trends in labor force participation rates. Combining these factors with an examination of Moroccan legislation and legal practice completes the picture, demonstrating how the king, legislature, and judges have responded to societal change, and thus how the law has both impacted and been influenced by the economic and social changes surrounding the entrance of women into the workforce. While studies of such individual factors exist, as do comparative studies of a number of countries, there is no study of Morocco integrating all of these factors.

NOTES

1. Fatima Mernissi, *Beyond the Veil: Male-Female Dynamics in Modern Muslim Society,* Revised Edition (Indiana: Indiana University Press, 1987), p. 143.
2. Ziba Mir-Hosseini, *Marriage on Trial: A Study of Islamic Family Law* (New York: I.B. Tauris and Co. Ltd., 1997), p. 46.
3. International Labor Organization, LABORSTA "Total and Economically Active Population by Age Groups" (Geneva, 1998–2004), < http://laborsta.ilo.org/>.
4. NASA, *Continuity and Change in Her Work*, 2005, <http://quest.arc.nasa.gov/space/frontiers/activities/womanswork/chart.html>.
5. Mao Tse Tung (Zedong), *Quotations from Chairman Mao Tse Tung* (Beijing, China: Foreign Language Press, 1996), p. 561. Cited from "On Widening the Scope of Women's Work in the Agricultural Cooperative Movement," *The Socialist Upsurge in China's Countryside*, 1 (1955), Introductory note.

Chapter 1

Moroccan Family Structure: Religion, Paternalism, and Women

Religious and cultural values have shaped societal norms and ideals surrounding the role of women in Moroccan society, the household, and their entrance into the workforce. This chapter discusses Moroccan religious and cultural traditions to identify the basis of male and female attitudes towards women's roles in private relationships and public affairs. It looks at the Islamic religious tradition in Morocco, the role of paternalism and patriarchy in Moroccan households and society, and the impact of these two factors on Moroccan customs regarding women and work. This chapter creates a context in which to explain the changes of the colonial period and its aftermath, described in Chapter Two and Part II, and the job ideals and prejudices, covered in Part III, and provides a point of comparison for the changes that resulted from the entrance of women into the workforce, assessed in Part IV.

Islam in Morocco

Since the time of the Almoravid dynasty (1056–1147), which unified Berber tribes, Morocco has been characterized by adherence to the Maliki school of Sunni Islam. The Almoravids brought a strict Maliki tradition, which served as the basis for statehood and the legitimacy of their rule.[1] With the subsequent Almohad dynasty (1130–1269) came the "last great age of Andalusian culture," spurred by the philosophical work of Ibn Rushd (Averroes; 1126–1198) and the spiritual Sufi ideas of Ibn 'Arabi (1165–1240), which impacted the Sufi tradition throughout the Arab world for centuries to come.[2] When Christian expansion then dimmed the flourishing religious thought and evolution, an inflexible interpretation of Maliki doctrine began to characterize Moroccan religious life.[3] Maliki *'ulama* became a part of the state apparatus, and the Marinid dynasty (13th–14th centuries) built religious schools in urban areas so that religious learning would occur under state-sponsored and regulated institutions. These measures limited innovation and academic religious discourse, "fossilizing" religion in Morocco.[4]

Religion beyond the control of the state began to revive in Morocco at the beginning of the fifteenth century. At that time, Sufis became the leaders of tribal coalitions organizing against the Portuguese, who were attempting to gain power in the region through the acquisition of coastal ports.[5] *Shurafa,* descendents of the Prophet, took power, as Sufism had popularized the notions of reverence for genealogical descent and sainthood.[6] Sufi brotherhoods continued to spread and gain control through the end of the nineteenth century, when state centralization and competing Islamic movements began to lessen Sufi influence.

The teachings of Muhammad Abduh (1849–1905), his disciple Rashid Rida (1865–1935), and their *Salafiyya* movement began to enter the Maghreb in the latter part of the nineteenth century, as scholars and travelers returning from pilgrimages abroad shared their teachings and copies of their journals, *al-Urwa al-Wuthqa* and *al-Manar*. The *Salafiyya* movement criticized Sufi brotherhood interpretations of Islam, stating that a "genuine Islam" was needed to overcome European domination – an Islam that conformed strictly to the *shari'a*.[7]

Abdallah bin Idris al-Sanusi was one of the first Moroccan men to be inspired by *salafiyya* teachings. He returned from a pilgrimage in the 1870s and began preaching about the importance of adherence to the *shari'a*. At the time, the *Salafiyya* school was so new and controversial that shocked *'ulama* forced him into exile for "denying sainthood and miracles."[8] Salafis nevertheless continued to filter into Morocco, and their teaching slowly spread as the French came to power in 1912.

In the early years of the twentieth century, the state began to grow stronger as well, and the *'ulama* lost control of both the court system and education. The Moroccan population became increasingly urbanized and literate, and thus Sufi brotherhoods continued to decline. This decline became more marked with French colonization.[9] Islam, however, continued to have a strong influence on Moroccan society and family life.

Family Law

Moroccan Family Law is based upon the teachings of the Maliki school of Sunni Islam. According to Maliki teachings, men hold power over their female relatives.[10] Fatima Mernissi explains this male dominance as a fear of succumbing to the temptations of women, a fear the Prophet himself experienced. As a result, much of Muslim society is protective of their women, attempting to curb active feminine sexuality and prevent female self-determination in order to maintain family honor.[11] For example, Malikis require a guardian for a woman's first marriage, meaning that she is not allowed to marry for herself. Her father or legal guardian must arrange the marriage contract, an event for which the bride need not be present. This is different from the Hanafi school, in which women can marry by themselves.[12] Marriage itself is fundamentally "a contract in which a man gives a bride price and commits to supporting her, and in return, the man has the right to have sexual relations with her." The man's support is called *nafaqa* and includes providing for the basic needs of food, lodging, clothing, and medical care in times of sickness. A woman is entitled to these benefits after she consummates the marriage as long as she remains obedient and sexually available.[13] As these requirements suggest, emotional attachment is not an integral part of the marriage union.

Laws allowing polygamy and ease of repudiation further diminish emphasis on an emotional connection between marriage partners. According to Maliki law (and the other three schools of Islamic law as well, for that matter), a man can unilaterally repudiate his wife by repeating the phrase, "I repudiate thee" three times. Traditionally, this phrase had to be uttered on three different occasions, each three or four months apart in order to provide time for re-consideration. In the Maghreb, however, this process was shortened so that the man could repeat the phrase three times in one instance and be divorced. The woman had no legal recourse to counter such repudiation. In Maliki law, divorce can also be obtained by two other means: first, the couple can "negotiate" repudiation if the desire for divorce is mutual, and second, the woman can appeal to a *qadi* (religious judge) to dissolve the marriage. According to Maliki law, a woman can obtain such a divorce in four different situations: 1) her husband has a serious physical or mental illness or sexual problem that he did not reveal prior to marriage, 2) the husband is absent for unknown or illegitimate reasons for a period of one to four years, depending on the circumstances, 3) the husband fails to support his family while he has the means to do so, or 4) the husband physically abuses his wife.[14]

While this right to appeal for divorce gives women of the Maliki school more recourse than those of the Hanafi, a woman must provide convincing evidence for her claims, and ultimately, her fate is in the hands of the *qadi*. Men have a substantial advantage over women, therefore, in the realm of divorce.

Maliki family law regarding property also favors men. Property remains separate throughout marriage. A wife has control over her own assets, but her husband is the main breadwinner and controls how his salary is spent on the family. A wife cannot intervene in the way her husband spends his income as long as she receives food, housing, clothing and furnishings. Since a husband can choose whether or not to allow his wife to appear in public or work, a woman is at the mercy of her husband with respect to household finances. In addition, inheritance laws favor male relatives as men get twice as much as their female counterparts.[15]

As evinced by its marriage, divorce, property and inheritance laws, Maliki Islam has set the stage for a male-dominated society in which women have minimal legal power to arrange their own familial affairs. This has carried over into other, non-legal facets of Moroccan society, as well.

Patriarchy in Moroccan Society

Jennifer Olmsted defines patriarchy as "a system where men dominate women, primarily through the enforcement of strict gender-role ideologies, with the argument that women are responsible for reproductive labor and are more limited in their access to the public sphere."[16] Such classical patriarchy centers on the household and is common in peasant and agrarian societies. In these societies, girls are given away in marriage at a young age to households run by a dominant father. After marriage, brides are subordinate to older women in the household, especially the mother-in-law.[17] This section discusses these patriarchal elements as they are present in Moroccan society in relation to the places of male and female children within the family, education, norms regarding women in public, and household hierarchy.

Since girls provide a constant source of worry about family honor, marry out of the family, and do not support parents in old age, boys are shown preferential treatment in Moroccan society as soon as the baby-naming ceremony. At the ceremony, which occurs seven days after birth, rural families traditionally slaughter a lamb in honor of a boy and a mere chicken at the birth of a girl.[18]

Privileged treatment for male children continues through the educational process. Although the Prophet stated that "the search for knowledge is the duty of every Muslim, man or woman," family practicalities and traditions stand in the way of educating women.[19] In childhood, boys go to classes and run around outside while girls often must stay home and help their mothers with chores, errands, and childcare. Later in adolescence, when boys continue studying and apprentice for a trade, girls learn household skills such as sewing, embroidery, or weaving.[20] Afterwards, women marry into a new household and continue their domestic duties while men go off to work outside of the house.

Societal norms against women in public spaces impact the differences in the roles of male and female children. The Moroccan value system leaves the public sphere for men. Mernissi explains the repercussions if women infringe upon this space: "a woman has no right to use male spaces. If she enters them, she is upsetting the male's order and his peace of mind. She is actually committing an act of aggression against him merely by being present where she should not be."[21] Family honor rests upon a man's ability to keep his women in courtyards and behind walls and veils, out of the public eye. The streets are for men, the roofs and the inner courtyards for women.[22] Traditionally, women were only allowed out in public on trips to the *hammam* (public bath) and to the tomb of a local saint. On these occasions, a woman had to receive her husband's permission and be chaperoned by an older woman, usually her mother-in-law.[23] As a result of such ideals, women were trained "to be entirely domestic so that they [were] unemployable and economically dependent."[24]

Patriarchal ideals also influence the power structure within Moroccan households. There is a clearly defined hierarchy among women in the household in which the mother-in-law reigns supreme. When a new bride moves into her husband's house, she must act shy and demure at least until the birth of her first child, when her place within the kinship group becomes more fortified.[25] Her mother-in-law holds the power to decide who eats what when, and knows everything that occurs within the household. In such households, it is acceptable for the man to love his mother and have sex with his wife, but he is discouraged from loving both women.[26] This situation makes women appear divisive to the patriarchal family, as wives who are not kin relatives look out for the well-being of their immediate families, as opposed to the unity of the whole patriarchal clan.[27]

Men and women have different roles in the Moroccan family. Traditionally women are in charge of the psychological and social well-being of the family and family life, while men are responsible for the material well-being of the family and for anything related to providing for it. The woman's role rests within the home, the man's outside.[28] There are purported psychological reasons for this divide, in addition to the religious ones. Men are viewed as more reasonable, rational, and in control of their emotions, while women supposedly have stronger sexual desires and are more likely to succumb to their feelings.[29] Women, therefore, require constant male supervision and cannot be trusted to support the family economically or go out alone in public.

Moroccan customs relating to women and work stem from both the patriarchal nature of society and from the teachings of Islam. In the past, only Moroccan women who needed to work outside of the house did so. Because of *nafaqa* and the value attached to the seclusion of women, all respectable men provided for their women. Therefore, women who worked outside of the house were those who had been divorced by their husbands and whose kin groups could not or would not support them and their children, or lower class women who had no men to look after them.[30] Such women were not respected, as Mernissi explains: "[in] class-conscious Morocco, the maid who has to go wherever she can find a job, occupies the lowest rung of the social scale, and to be called a maid is one of the commonest insults." Seclusion of women, therefore, was a source of pride and a sign of wealth, since only women married to wealthy men could afford to remain out of the public eye. [31]

It was acceptable, however, for women to work in the privacy of their own homes. This was, and still is the case in rural areas where domestic chores require women to spin wool, weave cloth and rugs, and help out with additional tasks around the house and farm.[32] Women also have the opportunity to earn their own money by raising livestock such as chickens, rabbits, or pigeons, which are then sold, given as gifts, or traded among friends. Selling handicrafts such as sewing, weaving, or embroidery products provides additional acceptable means for women to earn money. Any money earned through such activities is the woman's own to spend as she chooses.[33] While these activities do not provide women with a substantial source of income, they allow them additional money to spend on themselves and their children, without being completely dependent on the pocket money that their husbands dole out.

Conclusion: Islam, Patriarchy, and Women in the Workforce

The religious and patriarchal traditions described above represent the basis for the views of many Moroccans towards a woman's role and place in the family. Such ideals of the subservience of women, *nafaqa*, the volatility of female emotion, and the importance of keeping women secluded have impacted the nature of the entrance of women into the Moroccan labor force, the type of work women do, and how working women are perceived. In a society in which men could repudiate their wives at whim, women inherited less money, men ran the household, and remaining in seclusion was a sign of wealth for a woman, it is understandable that there were many obstacles to the education of women and their entrance into the official workforce. The following chapters explore the circumstances that have led to changes in societal norms regarding women and work and resulting shifts in government policies, family law, family relations, and family planning.

NOTES

1. Mohamad El Mansour, "Moroccan Islam Observed," *The Maghreb Review*, 29, No. 1–4 (2004), p. 210.
2. Albert Hourani, *A History of the Arab Peoples* (New York: Warner Books, 1991), p. 190.
3. El Mansour, p. 212.
4. *Ibid*, p. 213.
5. Ira M. Lapidus, *A History of Islamic Societies*, Second Edition (Cambridge, UK: Cambridge University Press, 2002), p. 328.
6. El Mansour, p. 217.
7. C. R. Pennell, *Morocco Since 1830: a History* (New York: New York University Press, 2000), p. 141.
8. Pennell, p. 142.
9. John P. Entelis, *Comparative Politics of North Africa: Algeria, Morocco, and Tunisia* (Syracuse, New York: Syracuse University Press, 1980), pp. 7, 8.
10. Mounira M. Charrad, *States and Women's Rights: The Making of Postcolonial Tunisia, Algeria, and Morocco* (Berkeley: University of California Press, 2001), p. 31.
11. Mernissi, *Beyond the Veil*, pp. 54, 60.
12. Lapidus, p. 855.

13. Mir-Hosseini, pp. 46, 47; Charrad, pp. 34, 40.
14. Charrad, p. 37.
15. *Ibid*, p. 41.
16. Jennifer Olmsted, "Reexamining the Fertility Puzzle in MENA," in Eleanor Abdella Doumato and Marsha Pripstein Posusney (eds.), *Women and Globalization in the Arab Middle East: Gender, Economy and Society* (Boulder, CO: Lynne Rienner, 2003), p. 84.
17. Deniz Kandiyoti, "Islam and Patriarchy: A Comparative Perspective," in Nikki R. Keddie and Beth Baron (eds.), *Women in Middle Eastern History: Shifting Boundaries in Sex and Gender* (New Haven, CT: Yale University Press, 1991), p. 31.
18. Susan S. Davis, *Patience and Power: Women's Lives in a Moroccan Village* (Cambridge, MA: Schenkman Publishing Company, 1983), p. 20.
19. Fatima Agnaou, *Gender, Literacy, and Empowerment in Morocco* (New York: Routledge, 2004), p. 85.
20. Susan S. Davis, pp. 21, 25.
21. Mernissi, *Beyond the Veil,* p. 144.
22. Charrad, p. 66.
23. Mernissi, *Beyond the Veil,* p. 143.
24. Vanessa Maher, *Women and Property in Morocco: Their Changing Relation to the Process of Social Stratification in the Middle Atlas* (London: Cambridge University Press, 1974), p. 73.
25. Susan S. Davis, p. 37.
26. Mernissi, *Beyond the Veil,* pp. 128–132.
27. Charrad, pp. 55–57.
28. Margaret Rausch, *Bodies, Boundaries and Spirit Possession: Moroccan Women and the Revision of Tradition* (New Brunswick, NJ: Transaction Publishers, 2000), p. 51.
29. Lawrence Rosen, *Bargaining for Reality: The Construction of Social Relations in a Muslim Community* (Chicago: University of Chicago Press, 1984), pp. 32, 33.
30. Susan S. Davis, p. 71.
31. Mernissi, *Beyond the Veil*, p. 143.
32. Rausch, p. 52.
33. Susan S. Davis, p. 66.

Chapter 2

Colonialism and its Immediate Aftermath

While tradition and religion have underpinned Moroccan values and customs, social and political movements of the twentieth century have impacted societal norms, especially those regarding the role of women in society. Morocco's colonial experience brought urbanization, industrialization, economic problems, and societal changes. With these shifts, women began to work both out of necessity and in response to the increased opportunity that industrialization provided. Later as the national movement grew in force, women's rights became a leading issue, and women entered the political arena. When the colonialists left, Moroccan society took a new shape, laying the legal and societal framework for women to enter the workforce. This chapter looks at the era from the start of French colonial rule in 1912 to the years after its end in 1956 by discussing the changes caused by colonial rule, national and women's liberation movements, and the 1956 Moroccan constitution and other laws relating to women.

Colonial Rule: Urbanization, Industrialization, and Societal Change

On 30 March 1912, the Treaty of Fez formalized Morocco's status as a French protectorate. As a protectorate, French administrators controlled Moroccan policy-making and external affairs, while preserving traditional institutions to some degree. The relationship between Morocco and its French administrators was limited in comparison with other countries of North Africa. French domination in Morocco was mostly economic, leaving the Moroccan foundations of political and cultural order intact. Regardless, French colonial rule effected far-reaching change.[1] The French introduced the concept of a business office, in which even women held government jobs, mostly, to be sure, in subordinate positions to men, as secretaries and typists.[2] In addition, they brought industry, which would in time profoundly alter the landscape of the Moroccan economy and society.

Within the initial years of the French arrival in Morocco, they developed a modern industrial complex for light industry in the country. Europeans began to invest in Morocco, and industry grew as traditional handicrafts declined. The new industry led to changes in the distribution of population and societal norms. Rural residents began to migrate to coastal cities to participate in the urban labor market.[3] It was at this time that women first entered the urban labor force. When industrial plants were set-up in Casablanca, they required female workers to supplement the male labor force.[4] These women had little education and were usually illiterate, but they represented cheap sources of obedient labor with agile fingers for textile manufacturing. An increasing trickle of female laborers ensued as women looked outside of the house to supplement their husbands' salaries by doing housework for the French or wealthier Moroccans, serving as vendors in markets, or working in factories.[5]

The Nationalist Movement and Women's Liberation

French economic domination and societal changes stirred nationalist sentiments within Morocco, as waves of nationalism swept through the Middle East and North Africa. Egyptian nationalist Qasim Amin published a book, entitled *The Liberation of Women (Tahrir al-mar'a)*, in 1885, and a subsequent response to its critics in 1900, entitled *The New Woman (al-Mar'a al-jadida)*. He maintained that "the status of women is inseparably tied to the status of a nation." As such, "a woman needs to be educated so that she can have understandings and a will of her own."[6] Amin used Islamic law to support his claims, maintaining that Islam was the first legal system to emancipate women and grant them rights. Legal and educational rights must therefore be allowed women in order for countries of the Middle East and North Africa to throw off their colonial rulers.[7] While Amin's publications came prior to Morocco's colonial experience, his books served as inspiration for women in Morocco during their nationalist struggle, which began in the 1930s.[8]

The Moroccan nationalist movement evolved as the younger elite grew frustrated, particularly over the fact that manufactured goods introduced by the

French threatened Moroccan producers, and over the lack of education opportunities within the protectorate framework. They composed a "plan of reform" in 1934, demanding change from the French protectorate.[9] The movement continued to expand during the next two decades until it reached a boiling point. The last straw came on 20 August 1953, when the French deposed Sultan Mohammed Ben Youssef (soon to be King Mohammed V), exiling him to Corsica and subsequently, Madagascar. An "all-out" fight for freedom and independence ensued, as the plight of the newly venerated sultan provided a potent symbol for the Moroccan nationalist cause.[10]

Women, too, began to participate in increasing numbers in the nationalist struggle. As Amin had written, the liberation of women was seen as an important prerequisite to defeating the colonialists. Thus women played an active role in the movement against the French, smuggling weapons in bread, fish and shopping baskets, delivering messages, leaflets and money, and writing about nationalism and the feminist struggle. Malika al-Fâsî, for example, was a member of two secret organizations, *Zaouia* and *Taifa,* created by the *Istiqlal* (independence) party. She served as a messenger and liaison between the party and the palace in 1952 and 1953.[11] In addition to such nationalist activity, she wrote articles calling for women's education and employment in *Majallat al-Maghrib*, which began publication in 1935. A nationalist and a feminist, she was the only female signatory of the nationalist movement's 1944 manifesto proclaiming the goal of independence.[12] Other notable women during this period included Latifa el Fellous, who ran a nationalist journal, Habiba Amor, who transported arms and caches for resistance, and Zhor Lazrak, who spoke on behalf of the women's nationalist cause.[13]

On 6 November 1955, Sultan Mohammad V returned from exile, signifying the *de facto* end of colonial rule. This became official on 2 March 1956. As Egypt's independence had inspired Huda Sha'arawi to discard the veil, many women did the same in Morocco. The predictions of the grandmother of Fatima Hassar, an educated member of the *Istiqlal* party, seemed to be coming true: "My grandmother told me: 'after independence, you will be able to take off your veil, because women will be liberated…'"[14] Fatima Mernissi's mother reacted likewise to independence:

> as soon as mother heard that Morocco had gotten independence and the French armies were leaving, she joined the march organized by the nationalists' wives, and sang with them until late in the night. When she finally came home exhausted from walking and singing, her hair was uncovered and her face was bare. [15]

From that point forward, based upon such ideals held by Hassar's grandmother and Mernissi's mother, women expected change in Moroccan society as promised during the independence struggle. Many upper class urban women stopped covering their faces in cities and looked for the liberties and educational opportunities that they had worked towards through their nationalist struggle. Like in Egypt, Moroccan women had fought in the nationalist battle and taken the teachings of Qasim Amin to heart, hoping for greater rights and liberties in conjunction with the struggle to defeat the West.

Family Law After Independence

The Moroccan Code of Personal Status *(Mudawwana)*, written by religious authorities and members of the Ministry of Justice in 1956 and 1957, left many nationalist women disillusioned. The *Mudawwana* was based on the Maliki school of law and its contents were therefore almost identical to the religious laws elaborated upon in Chapter One. These laws made it clear that a man was responsible for providing for his wife; the law did not grant women the right to work.[16] The Personal Status laws attributed a separate sphere of duties to men and women: men in public, women in the house. Marriage laws remained fundamentally the same as Maliki family law; some minor changes, however, were introduced. The Code set a minimum age for marriage at fifteen for women and eighteen for men. In addition, it restricted the guardian's right of constraint – the degree to which he could suppress a woman's refusal of consent to her own marriage.[17] Divorce/repudiation proceedings remained largely unchanged, although the *Mudawwana* required that a husband's repudiation be recorded by two witnesses. This record would then serve as a woman's proof that she had been repudiated.[18] Additionally, Maliki laws regarding inheritance and polygamy remained unaffected. These laws were enforced through the Courts of First Instance. Basically a civil court, certain judges in each Court of First Instance chamber have the power to rule according to the *Mudawwana*.

Although women received the right to vote in 1963, this was a largely meaningless law at the time, as the power of the king made the voice of political parties and parliament negligible. Thus women emerged from independence with a new enthusiasm to effect societal change but little immediate progress to show for their fight, at least in the realm of family law. A woman had no right to work, could still be repudiated at whim (with just a little more planning for the witnesses), and a guardian retained a say in her marital fate. It was not until economic, social, and political events of the 1970s and 1980s caused more women to enter the public realm and the labor force that changes began to occur in family law, societal norms, and law enforcement.

Conclusion: What was the Colonial Legacy?

Colonialism increased the rate of change in Moroccan society. It brought new industry, new competition, urbanization, and an increase in the numbers of working women. It also created unrest, nationalism, women's public sphere activity, and ultimately, Moroccan independence. Post-colonial Morocco was different, however, facing new economic problems and industrial competition. Women, too, were different, as some had experienced the struggle for independence and wanted more. Part II discusses whether or not women received the benefits and independence for which they fought, by looking at post-colonial innovations and their impact on women in terms of educational, economic, societal, and legal change.

NOTES

1. Entelis, pp. 17, 18.
2. Mernissi, *Beyond the Veil*, p. 146.
3. Rausch, p. 56.
4. Rahma Bourqia, "Gender and Employment in Moroccan Textile Industries," in Carol Miller and Jessica Vivian (eds.), *Women's Employment in the Textile Manufacturing Sectors of Bangladesh and Morocco* (Geneva Switzerland: UNRISD and UNDP, 2002), p. 66.
5. Rausch, p. 64.
6. Qasim Amin, *The Liberation of Women*, trans. Samiha Sidhom Peterson (Cairo: American University of Cairo Press, 1992), pp. 6, 13.
7. *Ibid*, p. 7.
8. Fatima Mernissi, *Dreams of Trespass: Tales of a Harem Girlhood* (Reading, Massachusetts: Addison-Wesley Publishing Company, Inc., 1994), p. 121. Mernissi describes her mother's love for hearing the writings of Amin in Morocco during the 1930s.

9. Hourani, p. 329.

10. Entelis, p. 33.

11. Zakya Daoud, *Feminisme et Politique au Maghreb: Sept Décennies de Lutte* (Casablanca: Editions Eddif, 1996), p. 253.

12. Rausch, p. 65.

13. Daoud, p. 253.

14. *Ibid*, p. 249.

15. Mernissi, *Dreams of Trespass*, p. 120.

16. Mernissi, *Beyond the Veil*, p. 148.

17. Mir-Hosseini, pp. 26, 27.

18. Charrad, p. 165.

PART II

EDUCATION, ECONOMY, AND LAW – WOMEN GO TO WORK

Chapter 3

Educational Policy and Female Literacy

In *Beyond the Veil*, Fatima Mernissi explains that "access to education seems to have an immediate, tremendous impact on women's perception of themselves, their reproductive roles, and their social mobility expectations."[1] As such, shifts in Moroccan educational policy towards women in the wake of independence impacted the entrance of women into the Moroccan workforce. As women gained knowledge, they grew more confident and skillful and were thus more prepared and competitive applicants for jobs in the public sphere. Societal attitudes, however, did not change so quickly. Even men who favored educating women in theory did not educate their wives and daughters in large numbers. In spite of this, more women did manage to gain at least a basic education, making them more employable, independent, and likely to work outside of the house. This chapter examines the history and societal factors surrounding the education of women in Morocco by first covering changes in Moroccan educational policy from the late nineteenth to the late twentieth century and then discussing Fatima Agnaou's findings regarding societal and familial factors that have prevented many women from becoming literate and gaining an education.

The History of Women's Education

The first schools in Morocco to admit women were private schools founded by the Jewish and French communities. There were two girls' primary schools in Tetouan founded by the Jews and the French in 1864 and 1916, respectively. In 1921, Salafi activists initiated the first schools of the "Free School Movement" in Fez. These schools, though not free in cost, were free of French influence and control. Schools in Rabat, Salé, Casablanca, Tetouan, Marrakesh, and Kénitra followed those in Fez, providing the students with an education in geography, mathematics, and sometimes science, alongside teachings of ethics, the Quran, *hadith*, and Islamic history, all in Arabic. Emphasizing pride in Islamic values, these schools served to spread nationalist ideals of overcoming French and western domination via education. However, they were for boys only.[2]

In the 1930s, the French protectorate government developed the first public schools in Morocco – a primary school for boys in Salé in 1931 and one for girls in Fez in 1936. By 1938, there were eight public primary schools for girls. The number of women in school increased over the following decade. In 1945, twelve Moroccan girls entered secondary school; in 1946, 193 did, and in 1947, 7000 girls began their secondary education.[3]

The nationalist movement funded its own schools in the 1940s to compete with the French ones. The language of learning in these schools was Arabic and they, too, were open to both boys and girls. Such co-education coincided with nationalist calls to educate women as a potential means of defeating the French.[4] Once the French had departed, efforts to educate women began in earnest. The Moroccan government initiated its first literacy campaign in 1956, with the hopes of intellectually liberating the people of the countryside, creating a new language policy, and establishing a new political order. The literary campaigns of 1956 and 1957 succeeded in educating 3 million men and women.[5]

Morocco's 1962 constitution guaranteed the basic right of primary education in a state-funded school to every child, and a 1963 royal decree made this education obligatory.[6] At the same time, the Moroccan government held adult literacy campaigns that targeted women and agricultural workers in certain regions of the country. The Ministry of Youth and Sports also organized a rural literacy program for illiterate girls aged ten to fifteen, intended to teach basic literacy through such relevant topics as child development, nutrition, family health, and family planning. This program failed to attract enough of the female target group, however, and was therefore terminated prematurely.[7]

A daughter at home was still more useful to many parents than a daughter in primary school, secondary school, or a literacy program. Many people believed that literacy and education were irrelevant to female children, as a girl's most important role would be as a wife and mother. These ideals, however, led to a new kind of education program for women, *foyers,* in which girls gained a primary education while also learning needlework and housecraft skills. The *Union Nationale de Femmes Marocaines* administered this program in the late 1960s and early 1970s in various towns throughout the country. At the post-primary level, girls learned more elaborate needlework and crafts techniques, making carpets and embroidery, which were then sold through the Union.

Parents preferred these *foyers* to schools, since they did not involve co-education and were viewed as more useful to a girl's future life. According to Vanessa Maher, parents saw such female education as a means to "push up a girl's bride-price or dower, because she will know how to keep a 'modern home', how to knit and sew and pay attention to vitamins; how to count money, write letters, tell the time, and deal with medical prescriptions. There its usefulness ends."[8] This explains why many parents withdrew daughters from school after they finished basic primary education. Thus, even though the government began to promote literacy programs, societal values minimized the impact of female educational campaigns. The female illiteracy rate remained high (see Table 1).

Table 1: Illiteracy and Primary Education Rates, 1970–2002[9]

	1970	1980	1990	2002
Illiteracy Rate (adult Female % of pop. ages 15 and above)	92	84.5	75.1	61.7
Illiteracy Rate (adult Male % of pop. 15 and above)	68	57.9	47.3	36.7
Primary education pupils % female		34	37	40	46.4

Source: World Development Indicators Database: http://devdata.worldbank.org/dataonline

In the early 1980s, the Moroccan government identified improving female education as a social priority.[10] It allocated symbolic funds to start a yearly adult literacy program, which would target adult women aged 10 to 45. Eighty-one thousand illiterate Moroccan women took advantage of the programs, though many could not see them through to completion because of duties at home. Fifty thousand more adults in the provinces of Casablanca, Fez, Marrakech, Agadir, and Oujda benefited from evening literacy courses that ran four hours per week for six months in 1986. The course was limited in scope, however, because of a dearth of government funding.[11]

Societal prejudices against enrolling girls in school continued to prevent women from receiving the same education as men. Such cultural biases were stronger in Morocco than in neighboring Tunisia and Algeria. From 1986 to 1988, 107% of primary school aged girls were enrolled in primary school in Tunisia.[12] In Algeria during this period, 87% were enrolled. In contrast, only 46% of the primary school age female population in Morocco was enrolled in primary school at this time.[13] This comparative lack of female education put Morocco at a disadvantage in terms of development and attracting jobs from abroad, especially in manufacturing, in which literacy translates into greater worker productivity.

The United Nations Educational, Scientific and Cultural Organization (UNESCO) declared 1990 the international year of literacy. At this point, Morocco's adult female illiteracy rate remained at 75% while the male rate was 28% lower at 47% (Table 1). In response to the international call, on 8 January 1990, King Hassan II promoted fighting adult illiteracy as an important part of the National Development Plan. He created a national committee to combat adult illiteracy, which launched a literacy campaign that reportedly resulted in 254,987 people becoming literate.[14] Additional private actors initiated campaigns at this time as well, increasing the overall societal focus on literacy. These efforts continued as the Moroccan government formed an adult literacy department in the Social Affairs Directorate in January 1991 and the Adult Literacy Directorate in 1997 to oversee the creation of more literacy programs. The Directorate created literacy programs specifically directed at adult women who were not primary wage earners and had limited formal education. While many women enrolled, there was a high dropout rate of 72.24% from these programs, and in the end, the campaign only impacted 28% of the target population.[15] Nevertheless, the programs had some success, as by 2002, the illiteracy rate had decreased an additional 13.4% from its 1990 level, to 61.7% (Table 1). This improvement most likely resulted from the combination of the monarchy's programs and the increase in female primary school enrollment over the previous decades.

The government's continuous efforts to provide literacy programs and basic education to women, therefore, resulted in noticeable increases in female literacy. From 1970 to 2002, the female illiteracy rate decreased by 30.3%. As the percentage of female primary education pupils increased by only 12.4% in this period (Table 1), it is clear that the monarchy's literacy programs played a role in this decrease in illiteracy. Even with these efforts, however, well over 50% of the female population in Morocco remained illiterate. The next section seeks to explain the social and familial factors that impact female education (or lack thereof) in Morocco.

Why is The Female Literacy Rate so Low?
Interviews and Explanations

Fatima Agnaou analyzed trends in literacy campaigns as an indicator for overall trends in women's education in Morocco. She focused on literacy because of its importance in the empowerment of, and future prospects for women. Agnaou defines literacy as "an empowering skill [that] extends the cognitive and functional knowledge of reading, writing and mathematics. It is a process of reflecting critically upon one's situation within society and acting collectively with the object of changing what is repressive about it."[16] Illiteracy, in contrast, is linked to poverty, isolation, and subordination. Agnaou interviewed 279 participants in Morocco's 1998 literacy campaign to explain why women and girls often do not receive the education necessary to become literate, even with the government's extensive literacy efforts.

Of Agnaou's informants, 53% did not attend formal primary school, and the remaining 47% had dropped out as children – hence their need to enroll in a literacy course.[17] These women gave a variety of reasons for leaving school, the most common being parental opposition to education. Forty percent of the women interviewed provided this as the reason that they did not enter or left school. Twenty percent said that schools were too distant or unavailable, 17% gave school failure as a reason, 13% personally refused to go, 8% did not complete school for economic reasons, and 2% were denied education due to administrative problems such as the lack of a birth certificate. Poverty and the need to help around the house, lack of money in the town to fund schools, and language difficulties were also common reasons that these women could not receive an education as a child.[18]

The nature of school textbooks impact the way women view their education and their perceived role in society, both in primary school and during the literacy programs studied. The textbooks used in the literacy programs featured 65% male and 35% female characters in stories and drawings. In the books, women were depicted in familial and domestic duties or in limited occupational activities that were mostly extensions of women's traditional domestic roles and earned little money. Women also appeared as beggars or sources of entertainment in some textbooks. Throughout the books, female characters were portrayed as insecure married women who only gained legitimacy by having children (especially boys). One excerpt from a literacy textbook exemplifies these stereotypes: "She wants to have a fifth child to ensure her husband's commitment so as not to repudiate her." Another excerpt deals with the plight of a widowed woman: "Since her husband's death, she has become helpless and pessimistic."[19] As these quotes demonstrate, literacy textbooks have not served to alter social stereotypes regarding women. Instead, they have used such stereotypes to exemplify the role of women in society, even though the stereotypes may conflict directly with the empowerment and educational goals of female literacy.

Due to important domestic duties as mothers, wives, and daughters, many women that Agnaou studied did not complete the literacy program. Such pulls are the same factors that prevent women from receiving a primary education in the first place. Agnaou explains the sentiments of literacy program dropouts: "On the whole, they report that they are involved in priorities of life, which do not include literacy and many have the feeling that it is too late to learn and to read."[20] Domestic duties such as feeding children or earning extra money for the family hinder a woman's ability to continue with a literacy program. Thus, the necessity to work and earn money right now may hurt a woman's long-term education and job prospects. Women also dropped out of the literacy program because of harassment encountered along the walk to and from the classroom, which sometimes occurred after dark. In other cases, jealous mother-in-laws, sister-in-laws, or husbands prevented women from continuing their literacy education.[21]

A World Bank report corroborates Agnaou's findings that household and familial responsibilities, poverty, and societal values all hinder a woman's prospects for receiving an education. These responsibilities begin as young girls must fetch water and carry wood for their families. Depending on the distance that a daughter must travel to complete these chores, such duties can lower the rate of female schooling anywhere from 29% to 42%. These two tasks have no impact on male education, which is more highly valued in Moroccan society.[22] Thus throughout life, many Moroccan women have chores and responsibilities that are prioritized above education. It is only a fortunate minority whose families have enough money and are willing to make the efforts and sacrifices necessary to educate both their sons and daughters alike.

Conclusion: The Impact of the Educational Situation on Women's Job Prospects

Lack of education limits the job prospects for women and makes Morocco less competitive internationally for manufacturing jobs. Literacy rates in Latin America, East and South East Asia tend to be higher than those in Morocco and as a result, many companies prefer to open factories in those regions.[23] Within

Morocco, lack of education also makes women less competitive job applicants. According to Claire Griffiths, education is more important for a female applicant than a male one.[24] The statistics on the male and female levels of education in Morocco's urban workforce speak to the importance of education for women job-seekers. Twenty-seven percent of women workers in urban areas have an educational degree or equivalent, but only 14.4% of their male counterparts do.[25] Education, moreover, has a positive effect on a woman's chances of finding employment in urban areas. Gender discrimination is lowest in sectors that require the highest education. In these areas, 69 women are employed for every 100 men.[26] Women who manage to gain an education, therefore, are at a great advantage over their illiterate sisters in the search for jobs and livelihood. It is difficult, however, for women to gain this basic education in a society in which their roles as wives, mothers, and daughters interfere with their role as student.

The better-off families are generally the ones that can afford to forgo the labor a daughter can provide at home and send her to school instead. While women get better grades in school than their male classmates, society still does not sufficiently value female education.[27] This is evinced by the disparity in male and female literacy rates. Only education that is viewed as helping a woman better perform her household duties is seen as necessary, and even this education is a luxury that many families cannot afford. When a woman manages to gain an education in Morocco her chances of succeeding in the workforce increase substantially, but too often, she is not given the opportunity to obtain this educational advantage. Nevertheless, since the end of the colonial era there has been a noticeable increase in women's education as more opportunities have become available and the government pushes for change. These small steps have made Morocco's manufacturing industry more competitive in world markets and Moroccan women more competitive in the Moroccan labor force. Increasing female education has, therefore, favorably impacted the entrance of women into the Moroccan workforce. Educational programs, however, have created tension with existing societal norms and a sometimes difficult economic climate, in which families cannot necessarily afford to send their female members to school. The next chapter examines this economic situation more in-depth to determine how it impacted the entrance of Moroccan women into the workforce.

NOTES

1. Mernissi, *Beyond the Veil*, p. xxv.
2. Pennell, p. 186.
3. Rausch, pp. 68, 69.
4. Mernissi, *Beyond the Veil*, p. 154.
5. Agnaou, p. 49.
6. Claire Griffiths, "Social Development and Women in Africa: The Case of Morocco," *Journal of Gender Studies*, 5, Issue 1 (March 1996), p. 68.
7. Agnaou, p. 50.
8. Maher, pp. 83, 84.
9. Numbers for literacy rates from the year 2000 are currently unavailable from the World Bank Database.
10. Griffiths, p. 64.
11. Agnaou, p. 51.
12. The over 100% number means that non-primary school aged girls were enrolled, as well.
13. Griffiths, p. 69.
14. Agnaou, p. 52.
15. *Ibid,* p. 56.
16. *Ibid,* p. 41.
17. *Ibid,* p. 80.
18. *Ibid,* p. 81.
19. *Ibid,* p. 160.
20. *Ibid,* p. 83.
21. *Ibid,* p. 84.
22. World Bank Study cited in Association Démocratique des Femmes du Maroc (ADFM), "Parallel Report of Moroccan NGOs on the Application of the Convention on El iminating all forms of Discrimination Against Women (CEDAW)," (Rabat, Morocco. December 1996). Forty-two percent refers to distances greater than 1 km., 29% refers to close distances.
23. Valentine M. Moghadam, *Women, Work and Economic Reform in the Middle East and North Africa* (Boulder, CO: Lynne Rienner Publishers, 1998), p. 72.
24. Griffiths, p. 77
25. *Ibid*, p. 76, from Direction de la Statistique, 1994, p. 374.
26. *Ibid*, p. 78.
27. Mernissi, *Beyond the Veil*, p. 156.

Chapter 4

Economic Changes Draw Women into the Labor Force

As the previous chapter attests, economic factors have had a marked impact on whether women receive an education and subsequently on the nature of work that they can obtain. The Moroccan economic situation has created both increased work prospects for women and a greater need for female income. As economic development has led to new industries and opportunities for women to work, increased female earning power beckons more and more women into the labor force. A mother's time becomes worth more than the value of childcare when she can earn more in the official labor force than at home. As a result, the number of children per mother diminishes, and the number of women in the labor force rises.[1] Massoud Karshenas supports this claim with a study that found that family income has a negative effect on female labor force participation, while women's earning power has a positive effect.[2] Thus women enter the labor force when family income decreases and an added source of income becomes more necessary and useful to the family's standards of living – when a mother or daughter's contribution at home is outweighed by her potential contribution in a factory. Such has been the case in Morocco since the 1970s.

This chapter examines the economic situation in Morocco that led to the entrance of women into the workforce by first looking at the economic downturn of the 1970s caused by agricultural problems and shifts in phosphate prices, next detailing loans and economic stabilization efforts, then discussing the impact of these factors on the structure of Moroccan society, and finally examining the influence of these changes on the individual and the number of women in the Moroccan workforce.

Agriculture and Phosphates:
The Economic Downturn of the 1970s

In 1970, 70% of the Moroccan population earned a living through agriculture. The products provided 90% of the country's food requirements and 50% of its food exports.[3] In efforts to industrialize and modernize, the Moroccan government modified the country's water policy in the late 1960s and early 1970s, taking into consideration the recommendations of a 1964 World Bank study. It began to focus on dam construction and irrigated land to bolster modern, export-oriented agricultural sectors such as citrus cultivation, vegetables, and cotton. The national objective, which King Hassan II officially declared on 8 January 1969, was to develop "one million irrigated hectares."[4] The new water policy came at the expense of cereal production, a staple of the Moroccan diet. As a result, the government began to rely on the import of cereal grains, which led to a negative balance of trade in 1973.[5] The impact of these policy changes on agricultural output was compounded by a drought from 1973 to 1975, which further diminished agricultural production during this period. By 1975 agriculture had decreased to 30% of GNP.[6]

Changes in phosphate prices combined with the changes in the agricultural sphere to significantly affect the Moroccan economy. Morocco was the third largest producer and leading exporter of phosphates in the world in the early 1970s. Shifts in phosphate prices, therefore, directly affected the Moroccan economy. International phosphate prices tripled from $14 per ton in the fall of 1973 to $42 per ton in January 1974. By the following year, they had reached $68. Since the state monopolized Moroccan phosphates and received most of the revenues from production, it planned to use the additional phosphate income to expand upon its 1973–1977 five-year plan and increase public investment by 340% between 1974 and 1977. The government went on a spending spree, increasing food and petroleum subsidies and public sector salaries. The state also created 215 new public firms and bought more shares in existing ones. As a result of these changes, government consumption increased by 100% in real terms from 1974 to 1976. [7] The economy grew a yearly average of 7.5% between 1973 and 1977, and annual GDP growth increased from 4% in 1973 to 11% in 1976 because of the public investment campaign (see Table 1).

Table 1: GDP Growth and GDP per Capita Growth 1972–1978

	1972	1973	1974	1975	1976	1977	1978
GDP growth total (annual %)	2	4	6	8	11	6	2
GDP per capita growth (annual %)	0	1	3	5	8	4	0

Source: World Bank, DevData.

This growth would not last indefinitely, however. Oil prices had risen in 1973 along with phosphate prices, but the government's spending policy did not reflect the fact that as an oil-poor country, Morocco had to pay for increased oil costs.[8] It was not until 1975 when phosphate exports began to fall in volume and value that the pangs of poor economic planning began to hit. By 1976, phosphate prices had returned in real terms to their 1973 value.[9] In response, the government cut back imports and public spending and aborted its planned expansion projects.[10]

These adjustments proved insufficient to turn around the Moroccan economy, especially with new pulls on Moroccan state funds. In April 1977, Morocco sent 1500 elite troops to assist Zaire's President Mobutu to quell an attack by secessionist Katanga rebels. The costs of this military expedition, coupled with a poor agricultural harvest, increased Morocco's growing debts and budget deficit. Unemployment swelled as the economy declined, and high birthrates seemed to negate any short-term economic improvement.[11] By 1978, the annual increase in per-capita GDP growth had decreased to 0% from a high of 8% in 1976 (Table 1). Moroccan families were beginning to feel the economic strain.

In 1977 and 1978, the government tried to quickly remedy the new economic crisis with short-term stabilization measures. The government attempted to limit the budget and current account deficits by diminishing demand and imports. Taxes were raised and public sector salaries frozen; the government tightened credit and reduced social spending, consumption subsidies, and the rate of public investment growth.[12] These economic changes brought about a decline in the economic and fiscal condition of Moroccan households by the end of the 1970s. Youssef Courbage explains the impact of the loss of phosphate rents and the government's subsequent policies on the typical Moroccan household: "For Moroccan families, most educational, social, health and military expenditures now had to come from their own personal budgets, rather than from windfall state rents."[13] As a result, women began to work outside of the house in greater numbers so as to maintain their families' standards of living.

International Loans and Economic Stabilization Measures of the 1980s

The situation for Moroccan families did not improve in the 1980s. Due to the agricultural trade imbalance, phosphate decline, and large development and military projects, Morocco became dependent on external loans from such organizations as the World Bank and International Monetary Fund (IMF). These organizations insisted on economic stipulations in order to stabilize the Moroccan economy, as the country's foreign debt increased from $985 million, or 25% of GNP in 1970 to $9.72 billion (52.7% of GNP) in 1982 and $25.02 billion, or 100% of GNP in 1990 (see Table 2).

Table 2

	1970	1982	1990
Morocco's Debt	$985 million	$9.72 billion	$25.02 billion
Percent of GNP	25%	52.7%	100%

Source: World Bank, Global Finance Development No.2, 2005, p. 368.

After the government's quick fix attempt in the late 1970s failed, Morocco embarked on a new stabilization program designed by the IMF in 1980 and 1981. This program involved plans for stringent government budgets from 1981 to 1985, wage freezes leading to a 20% decrease in the real wages of civil servants, and a reduction in food subsidies, which caused a 50% rise in consumer prices. The price increases sparked violent riots in Casablanca and other urban areas in June 1981, forcing the government to abandon the stabilization program temporarily in order to regain control.[14]

The economic situation continued to deteriorate from 1981 to 1983 for both domestic and external reasons. Domestically, the government had failed to reduce expenditures causing the economy to slow and unemployment rates to rise. Externally, high oil prices, a scarcity of international credit, and record high interest rates on the world market exacerbated the situation. By March 1983, Morocco was bankrupt and could not service its debt or pay for vital imports. The government was forced to take emergency measures.[15]

At this time, the World Bank and IMF became more involved in the Moroccan economy through a decade-long structural adjustment program (1983–1992).

The organizations operated according to the Washington Consensus. In the short term, this entailed attempting to stabilize the economy by curbing government spending and subsidies, increasing interest rates and prices, and devaluating the currency to stimulate exports. Over the long term, the Washington Consensus hoped to promote economic reform through liberalizing investment and trade and privatizing public resources and enterprises. This liberalization drive touched every facet of the economy as the government tried to remove as much activity as possible from state control, instigated new salary freezes, removed price controls, and reduced subsidies.[16] These austerity measures further affected the quality of life for individual Moroccans. The prices of electricity, water and public transport rose along with food and fuel costs, but this time, public protest did not obstruct economic restructuring.[17] By the late 1980s only basic foods and health products retained price controls, and low-income families felt increased economic strain. Their quality of living had sharply decreased in approximately one decade as the phosphate boom had dissipated into economic decline and state debt.

International intervention, however, managed to begin restoring the Moroccan economy by the late 1980s. In 1986, the Washington Consensus's strategy of import liberalization eliminated Morocco's restrictions on products that could be imported. This made firms become more efficient as local markets started to face outside competition. In addition, the government promoted exports by stimulating the private sector, creating jobs, and abolishing all export duties and licenses. The manufacturing industry grew, and with it, women's employment. In 1989 foreign investment became easier in Morocco, as the government eliminated the 1973 Morocconization law, which had required foreign investors to have Moroccan partners. As a result of these changes, the budget deficit declined from 12% of GDP in 1983 to less than 2% in 1992. Debt decreased from 123% of GDP in 1983 to 81% in 1991, and exports grew by 9.7% in value and 6.1% in volume between 1983 and 1991 as the manufacturing industry took off.[18] International intervention, therefore, impacted the structure of the Moroccan economy and consequently, living standards and work practices in Moroccan society. The next section discusses the processes of urbanization and migration that resulted from the economic changes of the mid-1970s through early 1990s.

Urbanization and Labor Migration:
New Social Structure and Changing Norms

Changes in the structure of Moroccan society began after independence as the percentage of the population working in agriculture decreased from 78.1% in 1960 to 43.1% in 1982. Likewise, the rural population decreased from 70.7% in 1960 to 53.9% in 1989. The shift away from agriculture led to increasing employment in such urban sectors as industry, construction, transportation, communication, services and government. Between 1965 and 1980, the industry sector increased by 6.1%, manufacturing grew by 5.9%, while agriculture only expanded by 2.4%. As a result of industrialization, real GDP grew an average of 6.5% per year from 1956 to the mid 1970s, and per capita income increased at a rate of 2% per year.[10]

The changes in the Moroccan economy that occurred after the phosphate boom and international restructuring programs also led to an increase in the rate of urbanization. The government stopped subsidizing basic agricultural supplies as part of the restructuring plans, and industries in urban areas grew at much faster rates than those in rural areas. The percentage of the population living in urban centers increased from 34.4% in 1970 to 41.2% in 1980, to 49.4% in 1990 and to 55.2% by 2000, as people flocked to urban jobs (see Table 3).

Table 3: Moroccan Urban and Rural Population

	1970	1980	1990	2000
% of Population in Urban Centers	34.4%	41.2%	48.4%	55.2%
Number of People in Urban Areas (millions)	5.3	8.0	11.9	15.8
Number of People in Rural Areas (millions)	10.1	11.4	12.7	12.9

Source: UNSTATS, United Nations Statistical Database, 19 July 2005, <http://unstats.un.org/unsd>.

As a result of rural to urban migration, the economically active population grew on average 0.8% annually in rural areas and 3.8% annually in urban areas between 1985 and 1993. This growth occurred faster than population growth, which was only 0.4% and 3.4% in rural and urban areas respectively, as a result of the age structure of the population and labor migration from rural to urban areas.[20]

Approximately 1.1 million Moroccans migrated to Europe for work between 1971 and 1982, as well. Men accounted for the bulk of the migration until the oil crisis of the mid-1970s. After economic stabilization measures began in the mid-1980s, increasing numbers of Moroccan women migrated to such European destinations as Spain, Italy and France, and Arab countries including Libya and the Gulf States. Some of these women migrated to join their husbands or other male family members, while others went in search of employment in the domestic sector or to escape broken marriages and social stigma.[21]

The possibility for women to leave not just the home, but the country, emerged from changes in the norms and social structures of Moroccan society. The rural to urban progression that began after independence instigated a shift in the societal perception of a woman's place from conservative rural ideals of women at home to a slightly more liberal, urbanized perspective, allowing women to work outside of the house. As men migrated from the countryside to urban areas, women assumed greater responsibility around the house and were no longer restricted to domestic activity. Ninna Sorenson describes one such shift in responsibility: "In the 1950s, for example, only men participated in the harvest. Recently, because of migration, many women have begun to take over this role. As a result, some of the younger men refuse to work in what has now come to be dubbed 'women's work.'"[22] In 1983, women headed somewhere between 17% and 22% of households in Morocco because of divorce, worker migration, or the death of the male head.[23] Without male household leaders, women took charge of the house and the day-to-day tasks of supporting and maintaining the family.

In the late 1980s and 1990s, women, too, began migrating in greater numbers to urban areas in search of higher pay, less tiring jobs, better infrastructure, and more social and educational opportunities. While some women met with marginalization, illiteracy, squalid accommodation and exploitation in urban areas, others gained freedom and better employment from their new location. The next section examines the effect that the changing economic circumstances and societal norms had on the entrance of women into the Moroccan urban labor force.

Economic and Social Changes and the Entrance of Women into the Workforce

Economic changes and social shifts that occurred due to urban migration help to explain the entrance of women into the Moroccan workforce in the late 1970s and early 1980s. Women could potentially earn more by working in an urban job than remaining at home, and family income in Morocco had declined, while female earning power increased. According to Karshenas's findings, as mentioned at the beginning of this chapter, this situation should lead to an increase in women in the labor force, which is exactly what happened in Morocco at this time. Additionally, as it became more difficult for Moroccan men to find stable, regular jobs to support their families, women were forced to work for wages outside of the home.[24]

There was a steady increase in the percentage of women in the urban labor force from 12.9% in 1960 to 26.2% in 1990.[25] According to the International Labour Organization, the overall rate of female economic activity for women over age fifteen more than doubled as the percentage of men in the labor force actually decreased between 1971 and 2002 (Table 4). Table 4 demonstrates that between 1971 and 1982, the rate of female economic activity increased from 12.6% to 16.9%, an increase of 4.3%. During the same period, the rate of male economic activity decreased from 80.0% to 78.3%, a decrease of 1.7%. Over the next twenty years, from 1982 to 2002, the female activity rate increased by another 8.0% to 24.9% activity, while the male activity rate decreased by an additional 1.0%.[26] Between 1971 and 2002, therefore, the rate of female economic activity nearly doubled with an increase of 12.3%, while male activity decreased slightly. This data demonstrates that women were entering the workforce at a much faster rate than their male counterparts in this period. Thus the rise in women workers was more than just a "natural increase" in employment. Female labor force participation had become more necessary and socially acceptable.

Table 4

	1971	1982	1990	2002
Male economic activity (% age 15+)	80.0	78.3	74.9	77.3
Female economic activity (% age 15+)	12.6	16.9	25.1	24.9

Source: ILO, LABORSTA Labor Statistics Database, 19 July2005, <http://laborsta.ilo.org>.

As the discussion above and Table 4 demonstrate, women entered the labor force in Morocco at accelerating rates between 1971 and 2002. On the economic front, the entrance of women to the workforce occurred because of the need for them to work, increased opportunity in urban areas through more manufacturing and factory jobs, and shifting social norms as a result of changing family patterns caused by urbanization and labor migration. Slowly increasing literacy rates and educational opportunities at the time made women more employable as well, and as the next chapter details, new social movements and laws protecting women's working conditions and right to employment added to the participation rates of women in the Moroccan labor force during this period.

NOTES

1. Massoud Karshenas, "Economic Liberalization, Competitiveness, and Women's Employment in the Middle East and North Africa," in Djavad Salehi-Isfahani (ed.), *Labor and Human Capital in the Middle East* (Reading, UK: Ithaca Press, 2001), pp. 147–194.
2. *Ibid*, p. 166. Family income and women's labor force participation are inversely proportional. When family income goes up, female labor force participation goes down, and vice versa. Women's earning power and female labor force participation, in contrast, are directly proportional. When earning power increases, so does labor force participation.
3. Entelis, pp. 77, 78.
4. Will D. Swearingen, *Moroccan Mirages: Agrarian Dreams and Deceptions, 1912–1986* (London: I.B. Tauris & Co. Ltd., 1988), p. 164.
5. Georges Sabagh, "The Challenges of Population Growth in Morocco," *Middle East Report*, No. 181 (Mar/Apr 1993), p. 32; Swearingen, p. 183.
6. Entelis, pp. 78, 79.
7. Guilain P. Denoeux and Abdeslam Maghraoui, "The Political Economy of Structural Adjustment in Morocco," in Azzedine Layachi (ed.), *Economic Crisis and Political Change in North Africa* (Westport, CT: Praeger Publishers, 1998), p. 56.
8. Entelis, p. 79.
9. Denouex and Maghraoui, p. 56.
10. Ahmed Rhazaoui, "Recent Economic Trends: Managing the Indebtedness," in I. William Zartman (ed.), *The Political Economy of Morocco* (New York: Praeger, 1987), p. 145.
11. Entelis, pp. 57, 80, 81.
12. Denouex and Maghraoui, pp. 56, 57.

13. Youssef Courbage, "Demographic Change in the Arab World: The Impact of Migration, Education and Taxes in Egypt and Morocco," *Middle East Report*, No. 190 (Sep/Oct 1994), p. 21.
14. Denouex and Maghraoui, p. 57, and Susan E. Waltz, *Human Rights and Reform: Changing the Face of North African Politics* (Berkeley, CA: University of California Press, 1995), p. 124, discussing riots and stabilization measures; Moghadam, *Women, Work and Economic Reform,* p. 52 on wage freezes; Karen Pfeifer and Marsha Pripstein Posusney, "Arab Economies and Globalization: An Overview," in Doumato and Posusney (eds.), *Women and Globalization in the Arab Middle East,* p. 42.
15. Denouex and Maghraoui, p. 57.
16. Pfeifer and Pripstein, p. 37; Sabagh, p. 33; Denouex and Maghraoui, p. 55; Rhazaoui, p. 155.
17. Denouex and Maghraoui, p. 58; Pfiefer and Pripstein, p. 43.
18. Denouex and Maghraoui, pp. 60–64.
19. Sabagh, p. 32.
20. Saâd Belghazi and Sally Baden, "Wage discrimination by gender in Morocco's urban labour force: Evidence and implications for industrial and labour policy," in Carol Miller and Jessica Vivian (eds.), *Women's Employment in the Textile Manufacturing Sectors of Bangladesh and Morocco* (Geneva Switzerland: UNRISD and UNDP, 2002), p. 40.
21. Ninna Nyberg Sorensen, "Migrant Remittances as a Development Tool: The Case of Morocco," *Migration Policy Research*, No. 2 (June 2004), pp. 4, 11; Moghadam, *Modernizing Women: Gender and Social Change in the Middle East* (Boulder, CO: Lynne Rienner Publishers, 1993), p. 20.
22. Sorensen, p. 10.
23. Moghadam, *Women, Work and Economic Reform*, p. 54; Louis Lief, "Motorbikes or Veils? Women in Morocco Now Can Choose," *The Christian Science Monitor*, August 25 (1983), p. B22.
24. Mernissi, *Beyond the Veil*, p. 149.
25. Sabagh, p. 33.
26. Errors or inconsistencies in data collection may account for this apparent decrease in the rate of male economic activity. It is clear from the data, however, that the percentage of women in the labor force increased substantially during this period, while the number of men decreased slightly or remained about the same.

Chapter 5

Laws, Social Movements, and Women's Labor

Although *Shari'a* dictated Moroccan family law, a combination of French and Islamic law provided the basis for the remainder of the Moroccan legal system. Under this system, women enjoy nearly equal labor rights to men. The legislation that regulates female labor rights stems from a combination of domestic laws and international treaties that Morocco has ratified.

This legislation has been influenced by social movements in Morocco. Since the beginning of the nationalist struggle, women have fought to gain and extend their rights in Moroccan society. These movements have helped to shape and expand the legal protection and liberties granted women at work and in other facets of daily life. This chapter analyzes how laws and social movements in Morocco affected the entrance of women into the Moroccan workforce by first looking at Moroccan labor law and next discussing relevant social movements in the struggle for women's rights.

Domestic Laws and Women's Labor

Labor law in Morocco consists of a combination of texts. Some deal with legislation regarding all workers and others speak specifically about women, protecting them from jobs deemed too physically demanding or morally compromising. The first and most general basis of labor law regarding women's rights in the workforce stems from the Moroccan Constitution, which was first adopted in 1962. Articles 8, 12, and 13 of the Constitution deal with women's rights to citizenship, public, and equal employment. Article 8 defines women as equal, voting citizens: "(1) Men and Women enjoy equal political rights. (2) All citizens of age of both sexes are electors, provided they enjoy their civil and political rights." Article 12 discusses public office: "All citizens have access, under equal conditions, to public functions and public employment," and article 13 grants all citizens, women included, the right to education and employment: "All citizens have equal rights to education and to work."[1] These general principles about the rights of women to vote, participate in public office and work, however, represent broad guidelines that are mitigated by more specific and restrictive labor laws.

Morocco's female-specific labor laws are intended to protect women from what is termed "Dangerous Employment." Many of these laws were written during the years just prior to or after independence. They define dangerous jobs as those that require women to lubricate or clean running machines, to operate machines with dangerous parts by hand, to run sewing machines with pedals if under age 16, or to inhale toxic fumes. Other legislation from 1957 seeks to protect the morality of women by forbidding the employment of women in the design or selling of anything imprinted with immoral or criminal images and by making it illegal for women to work in mines or racetracks. Additional protective measures adopted in the late 1940s stipulate the maximum amount of weight a woman can be expected to lift, push, carry, or pull, and specify the length of the workday and the hours that one is allowed to work. Typically, women cannot be employed during the day for more than ten hours, broken by a one-hour minimum break.[2] Certain commercial and industrial establishments are allowed to set this rule aside temporarily[3] or even permanently in the cases of radio employment, bars, restaurants, hotels, cigarette shops, and entertainment establishments, but the workday in these places may still not exceed 12 hours.[4]

There is also special legislation to protect children and pregnant women. According to a 1958 statute, women are entitled to take unpaid leave not exceeding two years renewable in order to take care of a child who is under five years of age or disabled, requiring special care. A 1966 decree allows female personnel the benefit of a ten-week paid maternity leave.[5] This was lengthened in March 1996 to include a leave of four weeks before birth, totaling 12 weeks before and after, as well as daily breaks to allow for breast-feeding.[6] These later changes however, occurred only after long battles for equality and women's rights, which will be detailed in the next section and a later chapter.

In terms of salary, women supposedly enjoy equality of pay, as Morocco adheres to the agreement adopted by the International Conference on Work concerning equality of payment for manpower done by either men or women for labor that is of the same value. In addition, an international treaty from the ITO convention no. 4, which Morocco ratified on 13 June 1956, guarantees men and women equal treatment in the event of a work accident. Thus, at least in name, Moroccan women enjoy labor rights equal to men.

Combined with the Laws of Personal Status, however, the labor situation in Morocco between 1970 and 1996 was not so gender neutral. At this time, women were considered minors under the guardianship of their husbands and fathers. The Code of Obligations and Contracts required a woman to seek her husband's permission before contracting for a job. This law was not amended until 1996. In addition, women were (and still are) generally not given the same types of jobs or salaries as men, even though the right to equal salary was stipulated by both domestic and international law. While many labor laws strive to protect women and appear progressive in terms of gender equality, legislation can only do so much to shape the values and traditions of society. Social movements, however, as discussed in the next section and in a later chapter, have managed to create deeper and more lasting social change – most importantly, amending the Code of Personal Status.

Conclusion: Fighting for Social Change in Morocco

All of this legislation on behalf of women is only as good as its enforcement and applicability. From independence through the mid-1990s, regardless of the formal equality afforded female employment, a woman was still at the mercy of her husband's wishes. The situation began to change in 1996 after years of fighting for changes in the Personal Status Laws. These changes will be discussed further in a later chapter. This section looks at the middle years of the women's liberation struggle between 1970 and the 1990s, which provided crucial underpinnings for women's liberation in the decade to follow.

In the 1970s and 1980s, as female access to education slowly increased, and female income grew more important to familial livelihood, many women became increasingly unhappy with their place in society. The divide between women's rights and their levels of education, literacy, and workforce participation inspired women to unite to protest the "gap between their abilities and education on one hand, and their inferior legal status, their lack of political representation, and continuing discrimination against women in education and employment on the other."[7]

Thus the entrance of women into the labor force both impacted and was affected by the struggle for social change in Morocco. As women workers became more vital to individual households and to the manufacturing industry in Morocco, women's voices became louder and people began to listen. At this point, in the late 1970s, the feminist struggle was launched in Morocco. This struggle was distinct from the nationalist movement's efforts on behalf of women in the 1940s and 1950s. The new fight for women's rights aimed to change women's place in Moroccan society without the previous anti-colonialist tones. Many women worked towards change through voluntary political organizations. The most visible of the twenty-nine political organizations in which women participated included the National Union of Moroccan Women, the Democratic Association of Moroccan Women, and the Union of Feminine Action.[8]

Many of the organizations faced obstacles because of political party control and state restrictions.[9] In addition, the membership of such organizations was not representative of the Moroccan female population. Only elite women were involved in politics, since a minimal level of education was required in order for women to present their demands or be politically aware at all. Regardless, these groups were vital to the struggle to amend the Code of Personal Status. Women would not be truly equal workers and members of society as long as their fathers signed their marriage contracts without their presence, their husbands could repudiate them at whim, and both fathers and husbands could prevent their participation in the labor force. While changes in the Code of Personal Status did not occur until more than two decades after the feminist struggle began, the increasing publicity that the women's rights movement received served as inspiration for more women to strive for education and better jobs and led the king to pay attention to the movement's efforts. As women's education and economic importance increased, their struggle for equality in *every* facet of Moroccan law became stronger and more significant, thus laying the foundations for the significant amendments to the Code of Personal Status and women's rights in Morocco that occurred in the late 1990s and initial years of the 21st century.

NOTES

1. Kingdom of Morocco, *1992 Constitution*, retrieved from <http://www.oefre.unibe.ch/ law/icl/mo00000_.html>, 2005.
2. Women are, however, allowed to work for 7 hours or less straight through without a break. ADFM, "Parallel Report of Moroccan NGOs".
3. This is the case for butter factories, confectionery, fruit and vegetable canneries, fish, cheese, and industrial establishments that treat milk, perfume, flowers, and green-houses for fruits and vegetables. *Ibid.*
4. Information on these laws retrieved from *ibid.*
5. *Ibid.*
6. Julie Combe, *La Condition de la Femme Marocaine* (Paris: L'Harmattan, 2001), p. 161.
7. Liat Kozma, "Remembrance of Things Past: Leila Abouzeid and Moroccan National History," *Social Politics*, 6, No. 3 (Fall 1999), p. 395.
8. Azzedine Layachi, "State-Society Relations and Change in Morocco," in *idem* (ed.), *Economic Crisis and Political Change in North Africa* (Westport, CT: Praeger Publishers, 1998), p. 99.
9. *Ibid*, p. 99.

PART III

WHERE WOMEN WORK AND WHY

Chapter 6

Rural Women at Work

"As a global characteristic, most women are employed in only a few industries (such as light manufacturing or services), certain occupations (such as unskilled or clerical), and types of manufacturing work (such as informal activities)," explain Zafiris Tzannatos and Iqbal Kaur.[1] This is certainly the case in the Middle East and North Africa (MENA), where women must weigh job prospects carefully against familial responsibilities and societal standards of appropriate behavior. The MENA region has the highest rate of gender segregation in employment in the world, and the rate increases as more women enter the labor force. In most other areas of the world, the rate of gender segregation is decreasing or staying the same.[2]

Such workforce segregation is evident in Morocco. Due to societal and religious stigma against women in public, female employment in the public sphere is frowned upon. As a result, women often find themselves in positions at work that continue the male/female divisions that originate within the family. Women who reach important positions in enterprises, institutions, and ministries are usually those in the fields of health, educational, and social services – roles deemed appropriate for women.[3] Even certain jobs related to roles typically performed by women in the familial context, such as hospital cooks, laundromat attendants, and bakers, are performed by men in public, since it is disgraceful for women to interact with strangers in the way that these jobs require.[4]

The Moroccan government took these societal norms into consideration when establishing professional training centers for women in Morocco. The government-run centers focus on training women in "appropriate sectors" such as sewing, embroidery, hair-dressing, typewriting, book-keeping, and musical education.[5] As the training available and social stigmas suggest, women are localized in certain sectors in the Moroccan workforce. Appropriate women's work varies from rural to urban areas, since societal standards and ideals differ between the cities and the countryside.

According to 1994 governmental statistics, 31% of women in Casablanca over age 15 worked in paid employment; in the rural eastern region of Morocco, only 17% of women had such employment. Nevertheless, Morocco's 1991 household living standards survey stated that 45% of the rural female population worked. This discrepancy is due to the income status of the work. The same 1991 survey listed 80% of rural women as family workers but only 10% of urban women in such jobs. The rural women most likely worked in agriculture and were not paid for their labor. This is one of the major differences between female workers in urban areas and rural areas: urban women usually get paid for their work, but rural women do not.[6]

Rural Norms

Most rural women in Morocco live in small, subsistence households, earn no personal income, have at least five children, and work around the house in various agricultural duties.[7] Such duties include caring for animals and processing animal and plant products, as the household's main sources of income originate from livestock, wheat, and barley production.[8] In recent years, as men have migrated in increasing numbers to cities, more and more women do the bulk of the family's agricultural work. Men may plant crops and later market them, while women weed and winnow wheat, strip maize-cobs in the field, fetch wood throughout the year, milk cows, goats and sheep, and harvest everything from fava beans to chickpeas to orchard fruit. Children assist with the harvesting, and girls often act as shepherds while boys are sent to school.[9]

Women can gain some extra income by selling eggs, weaving carpets from sheep's wool, and doing various other handicrafts around the house. This is not a significant source of income for the family but may earn money towards a dowry pay, for personal expenses, or supplement the family's seasonal revenue.[10] Most rural women's work, however, is unpaid and uncounted in official statistics.

Jobs that are Acceptable for Village Women

It is socially acceptable for rural women to offer domestic services to the immediate community. Women who have a skill such as mending can earn money as seamstresses or seamstress teachers. These teachers hold classes in their houses in which they teach young girls to sew. Their lessons serve almost as a finishing school, and the teachers generally have a good reputation in the village. A seamstress teacher must be rich enough to have room in her house to accommodate groups of girls as well as the education and materials to teach the necessary skills.[11]

Hammām mistresses also enjoy elevated status because the *hammām* serves as a hub of the rural woman's communication network. Women who enjoy such employment usually do not need to work but do so because their husbands own the *hammām*, or they want additional spending money.[12]

Overall, the village jobs that are most acceptable are those that require little contact with male strangers and occur in locations that allow women from the community to mingle with one another in a private place outside of their own homes. Whether in familial or neighborhood businesses, women in such professions usually do not need to work for a living but do so because of family connections, for fun, or for extra personal income. These are the most desirable and least labor intensive jobs in rural areas and do not represent the rural norm.

Jobs in Public: Dishonorable Work

Jobs that require regular contact with the public or other breaches of female modesty are looked down upon in the village. Field laborers, for example, are criticized because they cannot be veiled while doing their work since it is too difficult to breathe while wearing a veil and working in the field.[13] This sort of labor, however, is the most common way for uneducated rural women to support themselves and their families since no prior training or capital is required. Girls begin working in the fields at age nine or ten. Many are exploited and underpaid because women's labor is not valued as much as men's, and women are viewed as more timid and vulnerable.[14] In fact, employers prefer to hire women for many field positions because they represent cheaper labor and are generally more obedient than men.

Since the 1980s, women have also become more prevalent in public markets as vendors. This is a highly visible position in which women come into contact with male strangers. Debora Kapchan describes the new phenomenon of female marketplace vendors in the rural village of Beni Mellal:

When I first went to Beni Mellal in 1982 there were plenty of women in the marketplace. Apart from the vendors of wool, eggs, bread, and chickens, however, women were primarily buying rather than selling. The scene is different today. There are now so many women marketers in Beni Mellal that they have had to set up their goods outside the market walls. There is no room for them within. Women have also begun to hawk herbs in the *halqa*, the performance section of the marketplace. Their role as herbalists and their elaborate oratory in the *suq* mark a feminine entry into what has historically been a male domain.[15]

Kapchan explains that while the existence of women vendors in the marketplace represents a change in social norms, most female vendors are "socially marginal characters." They are divorced, widowed, or abandoned and are the main income-earners in their households.[16] Regardless of their low social status, these women are self-sufficient, and many people admire their work ethic even if they marginalize them socially.

Basically, any woman that must support herself through hard work or potential public exposure because of an absent or inept male guardian is socially stigmatized. Elizabeth Fernea depicts such views as she recounts a conversation with her Moroccan maid, Aisha, about a woman who had recently passed away:

'Poor woman! Poor thing! How we admired her, but how glad we were not to have her terrible troubles!' The dead woman's husband had earned a modest living sewing braid on djellabas, but he died young, leaving her with almost nothing except two small children. Her own family was too poor to provide for three more persons, so Fatima Kabeera had gone to work. 'She made very good bread and soup,' said Aisha, 'and took it to Djemaa el Fna and a man sold it from a cart and gave her part of the profit. She kept her family alive until her son was apprenticed to a djellaba maker, and her daughter sewed at home until she married her cousin...'[17]

This conversation demonstrates admiration for the woman's hard work and resilience, but the fact that she *had* to work in order for her family to survive is viewed as a tragedy. Even though Aisha herself is a maid, her husband is still alive and her employment takes place in the privacy of a nearby home. She considers her own employment much different than the dead woman's plight.

Employment in rural areas, therefore, is acceptable as a source of extra income but looked down upon when it results from the desperation of the need to survive. While attitudes in urban areas have similar foundations, as the next chapter attests, there are many more work opportunities for women in cities. The anonymity of the city and structure of urban life contribute to a more relaxed attitude towards female employment. Rural norms slowly change, but the ideal of a woman working nearly full-time around the farm while earning little to no income for her toils remains.

NOTES

1. Zafiris Tzannatos and Iqbal Kaur, "Women in the MENA Labor Market: An Eclectic Survey," in Doumato and Pripstein Posusney (eds.), *Women and Globalization in the Arab Middle East*, pp. 63, 64.
2. *Ibid*, p. 68. This is based upon analysis by the Duncan index, which looks at a scale of 0 (no segregation) to 1 (no men and women in the same sector). The MENA index number is 0.49.
3. Rausch, p. 108.
4. Maher, p. 112.
5. "Professional Training Centres for Young Women in Morocco," *The Xinhua General Overseas News Service*, 8 March 1979.
6. Griffiths, p. 74.
7. *Ibid*, p. 75.
8. International Women's Rights Action Watch (IWRAW), "Morocco," retrieved on 22 April 2005 from <http://iwraw.igc.org/publications/countries/morocco.htm>.
9. Maher, pp. 115, 116.
10. Moghadam, *Women, Work and Economic Reform*, p. 69; Maher, p. 115; IWRAW, "Morocco".
11. Susan S. Davis, p. 73.
12. *Ibid*, pp. 72, 73.
13. *Ibid*, p. 75.
14. Rauch, p. 70.
15. Deborah Kapchan, *Gender on the Market: Moroccan Women and the Revoicing of Tradition* (Philadelphia, PA: University of Pennsylvania Press, 1996), p. 29.
16. *Ibid*, p. 55.
17. Elizabeth Warnock Fernea, *A Street in Marrakech* (Prospect Heights, Il: Waveland Press, Inc., 1976), p. 214.

Chapter 7

Urban Women

The urban population grew by 153% in Morocco between 1960 and 1982, primarily as a result of the accelerated process of urbanization that had begun in colonial times.[1] This high increase in urban population was a result of better standards of living in urban areas, high rates of population growth, and more available jobs. Women had more opportunity to work beyond the confines of their homes in cities than in rural areas. This chapter examines the employment available to women in Moroccan cities by looking at the manufacturing sector, government and public office, the informal, unskilled workforce, and the commodification of ritual roles. Table 1 will be referred to throughout the chapter as a point of comparison for women in the various industries.[2]

Table 1: Economically Active Female Population in Morocco by Industry, in Thousands

Employment Sector	1970	1980	1990
Total Active Female Population	1595	2336	3108
Agriculture, Hunting, Forestry and Fishing	1216	1687	1986
Industry (total)	173	329	591
Industry (manufacturing)		322	579
Services	206	320	572

Source: ILO, LABORSTA

Manufacturing

The relatively large manufacturing industry in Morocco and Tunisia is unique among the MENA countries. In Morocco, it accounts for many of the new jobs in urban areas, especially for women. As shown by Table 1, the number of women working in manufacturing increased by 79.8% between 1980 and 1990, from

322,000 in 1980 to 579,000 in 1990. This coincided with a deceleration in the rate of increase of female agricultural involvement. The number of women working in agriculture had increased by 38.7% between 1970 and 1980 but increased by only 17.7% between 1980 and 1990. Many women who had previously worked in agriculture entered the private sector by taking jobs in manufacturing. The existence of women in manufacturing at all is a result of changes that have occurred since the late 1970s. Laetitia Cairoli describes this shift: "A Moroccan hired to work in a factory was, less than two decades ago, almost invariably a male; today, the Moroccan factory hand is almost as likely to be a female. The growth of the Moroccan garment industry accounts, in part, for why this is so."[3]

Manufacturing jobs multiplied as the manufacturing industry in Morocco expanded. They accounted for 98% of all female industrial activity in 1990. The growth in manufacturing jobs occurred as Morocco increased manufacturing exports as a percentage of total exports from 24% in 1980 to 57% in 1993.[4] This resulted from the restructuring of the Moroccan manufacturing industry and from economic crises in Europe, which caused European manufacturers to relocate production. Morocco presented a favorable alternative to Europe because of the low worker cost and facility of transportation to and from Europe. Before the arrival of European subcontractors in the 1980s, only a small number of women worked in the most unskilled, lowest-paid manufacturing positions. As women accepted lower wages than men, Europeans preferred to hire women for a wider range of roles throughout the manufacturing process.[5] Manufacturing, therefore, offered women increasing private sector work opportunities throughout the 1980s and 1990s. By 1990, 88.5% of manufacturing workers were women.[6]

Unfortunately, due to the global competition in manufacturing, women must be willing to work for steadily declining wages in order to retain manufacturing jobs. Although Morocco has a minimum wage, many workers accept jobs below it and remain impoverished even with long working hours.[7] Many female manufacturing workers are informal and therefore uncounted. They work long hours for little pay and are below the radar of Moroccan labor laws. As a result, they receive no social security, pension, or other benefits and may receive the same salary for both day and night labor. In addition, social stigma against factory work remains. Women in factories are viewed as unskilled manual laborers. The fact that they are willing to work under such difficult conditions implies a low class status and suggests that their male relatives are unable to support or protect them sufficiently. As one 27-year-old factory worker described, "people see you in the street and say that you are just a factory girl, that you have no value."[8]

Consequently, there are both pros and cons to factory employment. Although manufacturing offers women increased opportunity to work and earn money for themselves and their families, they are at risk of societal stigmatization, exploitation, and abuse in unregulated factories.

The Public Sector and Political Office

In the majority of Middle Eastern countries, it is deemed most appropriate for women to work in such public sector employment as teaching and nursing.[9] In Morocco, such public sector jobs often have shorter hours, may provide childcare services, and are more accommodating to domestic responsibilities than employment in the private sector. Public sector employers are also more likely to honor Morocco's maternity leave laws and hour restrictions.[10]

The public sector is not included as a category by itself in Table 1; other sources attest, however, that the percentage of women employed in this sector has increased since 1981. By 1996, one-third of state employees were women. As men moved from the public sector to higher paying private sector jobs, women filled many of the vacancies.[11] The increase in women in the public sector also came in conjunction with an expansion of primary education, since one-third of all state employees are primary school teachers, and one-third of these teachers are women.[12] The prevalence of women in education is a remnant of the French educational system, which favored women as teachers. Other than teaching, women tend to hold lower paid secretarial or clerical civil service positions, though as men have left the public sector, women have enjoyed better jobs.

Women have also become increasingly visible in politics since Morocco's independence. In 1962, of the 17,174 candidates for local political office, 14 were women. None were elected at that time. Few women ran for office again until 1976, when 76 of the 42,638 candidates were women. Again, no female candidates succeeded. Nineteen eighty-three brought more successful elections for women; 43 of the 307 female candidates running for local positions won, but at the national level, there were still no women in office. In the 1984 national campaign, none of the 1366 female contenders won their bids. These elections of the 1980s, however, marked the first time that women took part in formulating party platforms. Electoral television commercials included women, and women were subsequently admitted to the main party apparatuses, even sitting on executive committees in some parties.[13] Finally, in 1993, two women made successful bids for the Chamber of Representatives.[14] As of 1999, there remained just two women in the 325-member Chamber of Deputies in Parliament, two women in the 270-person Chamber of Counselors, and two women among the forty-one secretaries of state.[15] The numbers may appear to be meager, but through increasing visibility on the local and national scene, women were gaining a stronger voice and more influence in the creation of governmental policy regarding their rights and needs. Within a few years time, the process would produce substantial results (see chapter 10).

Unskilled Workers and the Informal Workforce

Most Moroccan women find their jobs in the unskilled and/or informal workforce. According to Griffiths, in the early 1990s, 63% of urban female laborers were classified as "unskilled or semi-skilled, non-agricultural wage earners."[16] Unskilled women are especially common in informal work areas such as short-term, home-based, part-time, or domestic work. Between 1986 and 1990, 70% of all new jobs created in urban areas were attributed to increases in self-employment, mostly through home-based family work among women.[17] The "services" category in Table 1 includes such unskilled women service workers. According to these statistics, the number of women working in services steadily climbed from 206,000 in 1970 to 320,000 in 1980 and 572,000 in 1990 – an increase of nearly threefold in two decades. This, however, does not represent the whole of the unskilled and informal workforce. Nor do all services fall under this category. As such, it is beneficial to look more specifically at one of the most ubiquitous unskilled, informal jobs in which women participate – that of a maid.

Maids and domestic workers represent a large portion of the unskilled and informal workforce. As more women leave home to work, and the number of two parent working families increases, maids and domestic workers are in greater demand. While Table 1 does not shed much light on the specific number of female domestic workers, Griffiths states that 114,000 women were employed in domestic and personal services in the early 1990s – almost half of all workers in this sector.[18]

Even though maids are becoming more common, they are still looked down upon and stigmatized by many in Moroccan society. Deborah Kapchan explains that "they are the *bnat l-haram*, the daughters of sin, presenting an explicit sexual threat to the woman of the house."[19] In the course of doing domestic duties, maids spend a great deal of time around the house and represent a foreign, sometimes unrelated woman with whom husbands may interact. The stigma associated with maids often results from this situation, as well as from the backgrounds of the women who serve in such positions. Many are older and divorced or former prostitutes. Others are young girls – either poor family members or indigent children – who work for wealthier families in exchange for being clothed and brought up as part of the family. Girls as young as four years of age are sent to cities as domestic servants to supplement their family's rural income. The plight of these child maids depends upon the family that takes them in. Some are brought up as the family's children, while others are abused and receive no formal education. As a result, they cannot obtain work beyond the domestic sphere after beginning as a maid, since they received no other training.

Informal sector employment thus offers women the opportunity to find jobs and supplement familial income, but the work is unstable, unregulated, and may be dangerous for those involved. Informal work is nevertheless a way for unskilled women to eke out a living, and employment in a home is preferable to more public, unskilled jobs as field laborers in rural areas or vendors in cities.

A New Twist on Ritual and Tradition

As men and women have moved away from their rural communities, traditional methods of ritual and interaction have been disrupted. In the past, for a wedding, birth, or other life event, members of the community would join and share their skills to henna the bride, cook, and entertain the community. As urbanization and labor migration have broken apart communities, women have made use of their traditional and ritual talents to earn a new type of informal living. Some of these jobs are highly respected since they are vital to the Moroccan lifecycle. A midwife, for example, holds relatively high status in society, as she enjoys a kinship bond with the children that she has delivered.[20] Others are looked down upon, as they involve public appearances or are associated with questionable magic. Musicians and seers fall into this latter category.

The public nature of a female musician's work makes her important to the community, yet marginalizes her at the same time. Musicians *(shikha)* perform at weddings and other ritual events and are central to many Moroccan celebrations. Kapchan explains the dichotomy inherent in the perceptions of female musicians in Moroccan society: "although they are central in their artistic function, they are marginal in society. As representatives of boldness and excess, they position themselves beyond the borders of social restraint...Stigmatization thus becomes society's means of controlling them."[21] Some female musicians have gained more respect and legitimacy in recent years as they have earned the title, *mughanniya*. This term signifies a more legitimate kind of musician, with a popular following or recordings. People who simply perform at weddings and in other ritual events, however, do not enjoy such status.

Seers *(shuwwafat)* hold a different sort of ritualistic position and may be stigmatized as well, but for different reasons. *Shuwwafat* experience "spirit possessions," acting as fortune-tellers and mystic guides for women. The women who partake in this profession are sometimes marginalized because of their societal positions as well as their associations with magic. Many *shuwwafat* were repudiated or divorced by their husbands after they began to practice, making their *shuwwafat* business their main form of income. Some have become successful businesswomen, advertising their services in magazines and charging as much as their reputation will allow. Women, especially those with limited spheres of contact to the public, consult *shuwwafat* as one of their only means of solving personal or familial problems. As such, *shuwwafat* fill an important niche, supporting and consoling women who may otherwise suffer alone. They offer an ear and present active ways for women to cope with their problems through candles, amulets, or spells.[22] Their association with magic and less than ideal family life, however, diminishes their repute and can lead to social marginalization.

This relatively new sort of informal workforce represents a realm in which women serve other women. As social norms and community organization become confused in the city, urban women benefit from the sense of community that women offering traditional services provide. Women in manufacturing, public service, domestic care, and informal work are all able to take advantage of these ritual services, since lifecycle events affect all levels of society. These unconventional "businesswomen" are thus able to make use of their skills, talents and self-promotion to create successful businesses in an expanding urban niche.

Unemployment and Gender Stereotypes

"There is no contradiction between rising female labor-force participation and rising female unemployment," explains Valentine Moghadam.[23] This was the case in Morocco in the 1990s, as unemployment rates soared for both men and women. The government succeeded in decreasing the unemployment rate from 17.3% in 1991 to 16% in 1992 by restructuring and privatizing many enterprises (See Table 2). This came at the expense of women workers, as female unemployment rose by 2% that year, from 23.3% to 25.3%. Male unemployment decreased by 2.3% over the same period, from 15.3% to 13.0%. Female unemployment rates continued to soar above male ones, by 1995 reaching 32.2%, versus 18.7% among males and have only decreased recently in 2000 to 26.7%, remaining well above the male rate of 19.9%.

Table 2: Unemployment Rates in Morocco by Gender in Urban Areas
(Persons over age 15)

	1990	1991	1992	1995	2000
Male (%)	14.2	15.3	13.0	18.7	19.9
Female (%)	20.4	23.3	25.3	32.2	26.7
Both (%)	15.8	17.3	16.0	22.9	21.5

Source: ILO, LABORSTA

Higher rates of female unemployment result from societal ideals marginalizing women in the work force and deeming men the real breadwinners, among other reasons.[24] Moroccan society considers female unemployment less important than male unemployment, since women are supposed to be cared and provided for by their husbands.[25] The Parallel Report of Moroccan NGOs on the Application of the Convention on Eliminating all Forms of Discrimination Against Women (CEDAW) relates one story on this subject about a group of 50 female engineers who approached the Democratic Association of Women in Morocco with a discrimination complaint:

> They reported that the recruiting public institutions excluded the female applicants and short-listed only the male ones for the interview. The figures they submitted to us are as follows: of 172 unemployed graduates of the Institute of Agronomy, 99 were male while 73 were female. The rate of unemployment was then (Oct. 1995) 11% for the men and 68%

for the women. The practice of discrimination in recruiting takes different forms: Married women are excluded because they are likely to have children [while] unmarried women are excluded because they are likely to get married soon. Some employers go as far as asking female candidates what type of male acquaintances they have and when they are planning to get married. Interestingly, some of the administrative figures (the Minister of Human Rights and the Minister of Agriculture) that these young graduates approached advised them to get married, the sooner the better. This discrimination is confirmed by the most reliable official statistics.[26]

This case demonstrates that even when women achieve high levels of education, they are still subject to societal stereotypes stemming from views about the "proper" social roles for men and women – the role for women being wife, not employee.

Gender stereotypes also impact the earning power of women when they do find employment. In a study addressing male and female wages and employment rates in Morocco, Saâd Belghazi and Sally Baden found that the average wage for Moroccan women was 23% lower than the average for Moroccan men. Moreover, 54% of female wage earners received less than minimum wage in 1995. The discrepancy between male and female salaries results from discrimination in payment and hiring practices, lower female education levels, the fact that lower-paid jobs are generally the only ones made available to women, and societal and religious standards regarding women and work. Since men are expected to support the women in their families, women in Morocco work either as a last resort to survive or because they want to. If a woman works to survive, she is desperate and willing to take whatever wages are available. If a woman works because she wants to, then the amount that she earns is not vital, as it serves as mostly supplementary income, and she is therefore willing to work for less.[27]

It is against these stereotypes and traditions that women entered the labor force during last 35 years. Some worked out of economic necessity, others for spending money, and yet others in hopes of obtaining more liberty and independence. Even though women in the official Moroccan workforce tend to be more educated as a group than men, societal prejudices and household responsibilities are often more important than education in determining whether a woman finds work outside of the house and where. The next section discusses how working women have impacted societal perceptions, effected legal change, influenced familial interactions, and altered family planning practices as they become more active members of Moroccan society.

NOTES

1. Belghazi and Baden, p. 40.
2. Data collected in 2002 used a different method of estimation and collection from the previous years and is thus not be relevant for comparison.
3. M. Laetitia Cairoli, "Garment Factory Workers in the City of Fez," *The Middle East Journal*, 53, No. 1 (Winter 1999), p. 29.
4. Noha El-Mikawy and Marsha Pripstein Posusney, "Labor Representation in the Age of Globalization: Trends and Issues in Non-Oil-Based Arab Economies," in Heba Handoussa and Zafiris Tzannatos (eds.), *Employment Creation and Social Protection in the Middle East and North Africa* (Cairo, Egypt: The American University of Cairo Press, 2002), p. 79.
5. Cairoli, p. 32.
6. Combe, pp. 163, 164.
7. Moghadam, *Women, Work and Economic Reform*, p. 62.
8. Cairoli, p. 37.
9. World Bank, *Gender and Development in the Middle East and North Africa: Women and the Public Sphere: Overview,* <http://lnweb18.worldbank.org/mna/mena.nsf/Sectors/MNSED>.
10. R. Assaad and S. Zouari, "Estimating the Impact of Marriage and Fertility on the Female Labor Force Participation when Decisions are Interrelated: Evidence from Urban Morocco," in E. M. Cinar (ed.), *Topics in Middle Eastern and North African Economies*, electronic journal, 5 (Middle East Economic Association and Loyola University Chicago, September, 2003), http://www.luc.edu/publications/academic/.
11. Moghadam, "Enhancing Women's Economic Participation in the MENA Region," in Handoussa and Tzannatos (eds.), *Employment Creation and Social Protection in the Middle East and North Africa*, p. 254.
12. Griffiths, p. 74.
13. Rausch, p. 67.
14. Griffiths, p. 66.
15. U.S. Department of State, Bureau of Democracy, Human Rights, and Labor, "Morocco," *Country Reports on Human Rights Practices*, 23 February 2000, Section 3. <http://www.state.gov/g/drl/rls/hrrpt/1999/422.htm>.
16. Griffiths, p. 74.
17. Tzannatos and Kaur, p. 67.
18. Griffiths, p. 74.
19. Kapchan, p. 232.
20. Susan S. Davis, p. 81.

21. Kapchan, p. 187.
22. Rausch, pp. 85–142.
23. Moghadam, *Women, Work, and Economic Reform,* p. 57.
24. *Ibid,* pp. 9–12.
25. Mernissi, *Beyond the Veil*, p. 159.
26. ADFM, "Parallel Report of Moroccan NGOs."
27. Belghazi and Baden, p. 44.

PART IV

THE IMPACT OF WOMEN
IN THE MOROCCAN WORKFORCE

Chapter 8

On Society

Women in the Moroccan workforce have effected and been affected by societal changes that have occurred since the 1970s. As working women have become more common, there have been shifts in the portrayal of women and acceptable female behavior. At the same time, however, many norms remain unchanged, thus taxing those women who break the mold of traditional behavior and leave the house to earn a salary. Working women are criticized by religious leaders and sometimes harassed as they commute alone in the streets. In addition, despite the multitude of literacy campaigns, female education leaves much to be desired. Just because women work does not mean that they have high skill levels. Over two-thirds of active women hold no degree and are therefore relegated to unskilled, informal, domestic labor.[1] This chapter looks at what has changed and what has remained the same in Moroccan society as women have entered the labor force.

Gradual Shifts in the Portrayal of Women

The images portraying women in textbooks, on television, in governmental publications, and throughout Moroccan society influence female self-perception and societal ideals of women. Shifts in imagery therefore impact the goals to which young women aspire as well as the support they encounter towards achieving them. For example, textbooks have continued to show women engaged in domestic chores while depicting men in important roles such as pilots, thus impacting the career aspirations of women. Other government publications have continued to display women in the home, while men are employees and active participants in society.[2] Not all societal imagery, however, has remained so stereotypical.

Television has been a vessel for portraying changes in the role of women in Moroccan society. While some TV programs and commercials display women at home, others depict them as managers, doctors, and lawyers. Both foreign and Moroccan women appear on television as newscasters and behind the scenes as directors and filmmakers.[3] The reach of television can have great impact on the pace of change in society in a relatively short period of time. Elaine Combs-Schilling describes how upon the occasion of the Prophet's birthday in 1993, King Hassan II used a nationally televised event in a mosque to project a major shift in the portrayal of women:

> One after another three men stepped forward who had competed and won in the poetry competition sponsored by His Majesty Hasan II. One by one, each chanted evocative poetry that sung of the majesty of the Prophet Muhammad....Then the ceremony drew to a close. A fourth figure draped in white, walked to the front of the mosque through the crowd of tens of thousands of men and stood beside the king. There were audible gasps; it was a woman... The white-cloaked woman, on whom the whole of the nation was gazing, recited in a strong voice the beautiful words she had written of faith in Muhammad, Islam and the Prophet's blood descendant ruler who occupied the central throne...She wore white cloaks, not precisely the robes of the men and the king, but sufficiently close so that the message was clear. She too was a part of the faith and citizenry. She too was a part of the white-robed body of nation.[4]

At a major national event in one of the holiest places in the country, the king broke with previous tradition by allowing a woman to pay respect to him and to honor the Prophet. This event confirmed the importance of women as Moroccan citizens, considered on par with men. While the 'ulama perhaps disagreed and other societal imagery still depicted women in a more traditional light, this was truly a moment that signified a shift in the portrayal of women in Morocco. After over two decades in which women had become increasingly visible and active members of society, it confirmed that the king recognized women as important citizens of the Moroccan nation, "its doctors, lawyers, mothers, line workers, accountants, scholars, air force pilots, agricultural workers, bankers, cooks, poets, parliamentarians, and maids."[5]

The significance of the king's shift in the portrayal of women only reconfirms, however, the impact that imagery can have on self-perception. By relegating women to second-class status in textbooks and governmental publications, women are still not afforded the same psychological and societal advantages as their male counterparts. This is also reflected linguistically, as

Moroccan women are commonly described by their relation to their fathers or husbands rather than by their achievements or professions. With the entrance of women into the workforce things have definitely changed, but there still lies a long road ahead.

Education: Cautious Success

With changing societal imagery and behavioral norms in conjunction with governmental literacy programs, Morocco's literacy rates have increased among both men and women. Since 1980, adult illiteracy rates have decreased by 20%, from 57.9% for men and 84.5% for women in 1980, to a male rate of 36.7% and a female one of 61.7% in 2002. This has occurred as rates of primary school completion have increased from 56% and 38% for male and female children in 1990, respectively, to 71% and 63% in 2002. Youth illiteracy rates, for people between the ages of 15 and 24 are even more promising as only 22.6% of young men and 38.7% of young women were illiterate in 2002 (See Table 1).[6]

Table 1: Illiteracy and Primary Education Rates by Gender

	1980	1990	1995	2000	2002
Adult illiteracy rate (% of people aged 15+)					
Male	57.9	47.3	42.4	38.2	36.7
Female	84.5	75.1	69.5	63.9	61.7
Primary completion rates (% of relevant age group)					
Male		..	56	60	67	71
Female		..	38	44	55	63
Youth illiteracy Rate (% of people aged 15–24)					
Male	42.9	32.0	27.4	24.0	22.6
Female	72.3	58.0	50.0	41.8	38.7

Source: World Bank, DevData

As the data details, however, gaps have remained large between male and female literacy rates. Among youth, while the gap decreased by 13.3% between 1980 and 2002, illiteracy rates remained 16.1% higher among women than men in the group in 2002. In rural areas, nine out of ten women are still illiterate.[7] Thus progress has been made, but much work remains. Women will continue to be at a disadvantage in the labor force and as active citizens in Moroccan society as long as they are less educated as a group than their male counterparts. Due to the nature of gender discrimination in the Moroccan workforce, women will need to become more educated than men in order to compete for the same jobs and salaries. Progress, spurred by the increasingly active role of women in Moroccan society, so far is promising. Perhaps as imagery and societal norms continue to shift, families will begin to value education for their female children as much as they do for their male ones.

Acceptable Behavior: Women in Public?

While acceptable female behavior in Moroccan society has not changed substantially as a result of the entrance of women into the labor force, certain norms have shifted. These include standards of dress and ideals regarding women and public space.

Women's styles of dress have moved in two directions as a result of the increase in female labor force participation. Some women have begun to wear more revealing western styles as they emulate western women by working and contributing to family income. Others have adopted more traditional dress, since they may have to appear in public to earn their income – whether out of necessity or choice. These women want to be less exposed when interacting with strange men and thus begin to wear a veil and more modest clothing overall.[8]

Changes in dress have accompanied broader shifts in behavioral norms. As women work for wages outside of the house for non-related employers, acceptable female public behavior began to change. Some women stopped lowering their gazes and refusing to talk to male strangers, as they began to view their role in society as not so different from that of their male coworkers.[9]

Not everything, however, has changed. Many women continue to feel uncomfortable in cross-sex conversations. Women in most circles are still expected to be more polite than men, and female interaction tends to be less assertive than male conversation. In general, women use more euphemisms and polite sentence constructions than men and are more likely to address people by their titles.[10] Women who must walk alone in public on their ways to school or work may also be harassed by "excited" men or religious advocates who view women alone in public as *haram*. Hence, changes in societal ideals and accepted behavior remain slow. Behavioral norms do shift as women gain more freedom through jobs and education, but change occurs at a snail's pace and is met with staunch religious opposition.

Religious Views:
The Path of Tradition and Shari'a

Some religious leaders are not too keen on the changes regarding women in the workforce. Ziba Mir-Hosseini interviewed family court *qudah* (judges) on this subject and found that in general, they were against shifts in the role of women. One *qadi* stated that "women's employment outside the home, and their apparent equality with men have upset the primordial harmony in Muslim marriage." As women work outside of the house, they neglect their wifely duties, causing familial tension. Materialism then replaces good, traditional family values, as women become "ambitious and selfish." They enter marriage with high material expectations "which are beyond the means of the husband."[11] As one may expect, the *qudah* believe that the way of the *Shari'a* is the true path and any deviations from it, including women working, disturbs the familial model.

Individual women have also encountered more direct Islamist pressure to change their dress and wear the *hijab*. This represents an Islamist response to the women's liberation movement, which has conflicted with the Islamist movement since its inception. In 2003, women began getting harassed for not wearing Islamic dress in public. A 20-year-old girl from the shantytown neighborhood of Sidi Moumen recalled the pressure she experienced: "It started with people spitting on me when I walked past, insulting me and my family. Then, one day in March, I was threatened in broad daylight by a man with a knife…He told me over and over: 'you are going to die because you are a sinner.'" She has since started wearing a headscarf and no longer wears jeans and a T-shirt.[12]

Islamist and religious responses to changes that have accompanied the rise in female labor force participation are not relegated to the social realm. The religious establishment has also reacted against legal modifications, discussed in Chapter 10, which altered the Personal Status Laws and gave women more rights. Every minor change in the public portrayal of women, increased educational opportunity, and shift in social norms that make appearing in public and acting as first-class citizens of Moroccan society easier for women is accompanied by a long battle and a great deal of backlash. For some, social change is too slow and contained, and for others, any change in the role of women in society is too extreme and far-reaching.

NOTES

1. Hillary Rodham Clinton et al, "Moroccan Women's Roundtable Discussion with the First Lady," (Marrakech, Morocco, 30 March 1999) <http://www.usinfo.state. gov/ usa/womenusa/hilround.htm>.
2. Rausch, p. 75; Fatima Sadiqi, "The Language of Women in the City of Fès, Morocco," *International Journal of the Sociology of Language*, 112 (New York: Mouton de Gruyter, 1995), p. 75.
3. Rausch, p. 76.
4. Elaine Combs-Schilling, "Performing Monarchy, Staging Nation," in Rahma Bourqia and Susan Gilson Miller (eds.), *In the Shadow of the Sultan: Culture, Power, and Politics in Morocco* (Cambridge, MA: Harvard University Press, 1999), p. 198.
5. *Ibid*, p. 204.
6. World Bank. *World Development Indicators Database*. Retrieved April 2005. <http://devdata. worldbank.org/dataonline>.
7. ADFM, "Parallel Report of Moroccan NGOs."
8. Kandiyoti, p. 36.
9. Rausch, p. 77.
10. Sadiqi, p. 72.
11. Mir-Hosseini, p. 126.
12. Isabelle Ligner, "Moroccan Women Fear Extremism," *Middle East Online – Women in Morocco* [Casablanca], 22 May 2003: <http://www.middle-east-online.com/ english/?id=5670=5670&format=0>.

Chapter 9

On Law

As women have become increasingly active members of the Moroccan workforce and society, they have fought to make their legal rights consistent with their role in society. They have formed associations and non-governmental organizations to fight for women's rights, published articles, and lobbied the king and the legislature for changes to the *Mudawwana*, the Code of Personal Status. Of particular note was the successful campaign in 1991–92 to collect one million signatures on a petition to the king to change the Code. Their struggle met with considerable, if slow-paced success, as the king set up governmental departments to work towards women's rights and integration, and ultimately reviewed and amended the *Mudawwana*.[1] This chapter describes the changes that took place in Morocco's government and legal code as women became more prominent in society and lobbied in increasingly louder voices for their cause.

Governmental Departments Dealing with Women's Issues

King Hassan II set up a number of governmental ministries specific to women's affairs. While these ministries rarely work in coordination, they have helped to prioritize women's issues on the national agenda. Women lobbying for social change and the human rights concerns of the international community have impacted the formation of these ministries and governmental divisions, which in turn have effected change in Moroccan legislation and the greater Moroccan population.

These ministries deal with issues of Moroccan women at both a national and international level. In 1986, the Ministry of Youth and Sport began to tackle domestic women's issues, specifically, illiteracy. Four years later, after the Ministry of Youth and Sport had enjoyed mixed success in pushing its literacy goals, UN agencies and the Moroccan government collaborated to create the committee for "Women's Integration into the Development Process." This committee served to link governmental and non-governmental parties with international organizations to finance socio-economic projects geared towards women. The committee aimed to more effectively integrate women into the development process and worked with the UNDP and UNIFEM towards this end.[2] In rural areas, divisions devoted to women in the Department of Agriculture and Agricultural Development as well as the Department of Public Health, have worked to improve mother and child health, family planning, and pre-natal care. Since the inception of both the Committee to Integrate Women into Development and the programs to assist rural women in the mid-1980s, notable progress has been achieved within the targeted communities. The funding available for women's causes within these committees and departments, however, has been insufficient to tackle problems within Moroccan society on a large scale. Instead, these groups have focused on specific categories of underprivileged women "in a disorderly, selective and limited manner, without developing any strategy, any sense of priority."[3] Such financial constraints and a lack of organization have limited the breadth and impact of these women's programs.

Additional ministries involved with women's issues include Morocco's Department of Human Rights and the Ministry of Employment and Social Affairs. Both of these departments deal with women's rights in the framework of international affairs. The Ministry of Employment and Social Affairs organizes Morocco's participation in various international and regional conferences on women's rights. It is also charged with sensitizing public opinion to the role of women in society.[4] The Department of Human Rights, which was created in 1993, works to ensure that national law agrees with the international agreements that Morocco has ratified. Within this human rights context, the women's issue is one of a number of general human rights concerns and has not received a great deal of specific attention. The department has failed to engage in dialogue with women's organizations and has not been particularly effective at promoting women's rights. The issue tends to get lost among all of the other human rights causes on the public agenda.

In general, the governmental organizations created during the mid-1980s and 1990s to address women's issues were not far-reaching in their recommendations or impact. Changes in the legal code detailing the rights of women and their place in society were necessary to effect true and lasting change consistent with the role of women as wage earners and participants in Moroccan society.

Legal Changes and Women's Rights – Beginnings: 1992–2002

Following two years of active parliamentary debate on contentious issues, including women's rights, the Moroccan constitution was revised on 4 September 1992. The revisions were significant in the struggle for women's rights because they affirmed Morocco's conviction to universal human rights. The preamble of the 1992 Constitution states:

> Aware of the necessity of setting its action within the context of the international organizations of which it is an active and energetic member, the Kingdom of Morocco subscribes to the principles, rights, and obligations resulting from the charters of the aforesaid organizations and reaffirms its attachment to the Human Rights as they are universally recognized.[5]

Women's rights represent a significant portion of universally recognized human rights. By admitting human rights issues to the preamble of the constitution, the government sent a clear message prioritizing human rights. Any piece of legislation that infringed upon universal human rights would violate one of the highest pieces of Moroccan law.[6] This includes legislation infringing upon the rights of women in Moroccan society. The 1992 constitution, therefore, paved the way for subsequent changes in the Code of Personal Status.

Beginning in 1993, a string of international conferences dealing with human rights and the rights of women moved women's issues to center stage internationally and put them on Morocco's agenda.[7] These included the 1993 UN conference on Human Rights in Vienna, the 1994 UN International Conference on Population and Development in Cairo, the 1995 World Summit on Social Development in Copenhagen, and the 1995 Fourth World Conference on Women in Beijing. In Morocco in 1995, however, women were still second-class citizens. They were considered minors, could not act as witnesses in court, and were referred to as property.[8]

The 1999 "national plan for women's integration in development," however, began to speed up the pace of reform. Introduced by the State Secretary of

Family Affairs and representatives of women's organizations, this plan aimed to improve women's medical, economic, social, and legal status in Moroccan society. Within two years, the true impact of the plan came to light as King Mohammed VI formed a committee of 'ulama and representatives of groups across the social and political spectrum to reconsider Morocco's *Mudawwana*. This committee included three female members.[9] The once seemingly sacred Code of Personal Status was to be updated to fit a more modern Moroccan society – one that included educated, active women as societal leaders and first-class citizens.

By the 2002 elections, change was in the air. Women were allocated 10% (32) of the seats in the House of Representatives.[10] In addition, five women won seats in their local district elections, and there were three female members of the upper house of parliament.[11] While this is nowhere near proportionate, as women represent half of Morocco's population of 30 million, it represented an increase of 1500% over the two seats held by women in the previous parliament. More groundbreaking change began with the fall parliamentary session the following year.

Breakthrough: A New Family Code

On 10 October 2003, at the opening day of the fall parliamentary session, King Mohamed VI announced a far-reading overhaul of the Code of Personal Status. While there had been minor changes to the Code throughout the 1990s, nothing had truly altered the foundations of Moroccan family law. These reforms did just that.

The new Family Code provides for greater equality between men and women. Women are no longer under the legal domination of their husbands or fathers after the age of 18. This means that they do not have to get their fathers' permission in order to marry and are no longer required by law to obey their husbands. The legal age of marriage was raised to 18 for both men and women, and divorce laws were altered so that divorce must now be obtained in court in order to be legally binding. This represents one of the greatest changes in terms of women's marital rights and status. Verbal repudiation in its previous form is no longer valid; repudiation now requires a judge's agreement and is only allowed under strict conditions. Women, too, can request divorce and have rights equal to men in divorce court.[12] Polygamy is also more difficult, and women can stipulate in their marriage contracts that it is unacceptable. In addition, paternity is now acknowledged even if a child is born out of an illegal marital relationship, for example, if the child is conceived prior to the wedding. Finally, the children of daughters as well as sons can now inherit from their grandfathers.[13] As compared with traditional Maliki family law, discussed in Chapter 1, these represent substantial changes, granting women many more rights in the familial realm than the previous code allowed.

On 5 February 2004, parliament voted the new law into effect, leaving it up to women to take advantage of their new rights and *qudah* to implement the changes. Implementation is now the biggest bottleneck in the process of increasing women's rights in Moroccan society. A Population Reference Bureau Health Policy Report explains that "it is also easier to change laws addressing women's status than to change the social conditions that give rise to women's inequality."[14] Social conditions have changed gradually since independence, with increases in female education and the growing number of women in the workforce, but changes occur at extremely slow rates. Time will tell whether the new legal rights afforded women will speed up the rate of social change. Such shifts in values and social status are not the kinds of things that happen within a year, or even five years. These are generational changes that will occur with time, complemented and reinforced by new educational patterns and shifts in priorities across society. It is important that the government continue to place emphasis on the women's issue beyond the realm of legislation, using campaigns to address the root economic, educational, and familial causes of the male/female divide.

Reactions to Reform: Islamism and Feminism

Religious groups, for one, have called for a halt to these changes in women's rights and status. They view any modification of family law as an affront to Islam and believe that the changes resulted from unwelcome international interference.[15] In an article on 21 June 1999, after the announcement of the "national plan for women's integration in development," for example, the League of *'Ulama* stated that "the nature of the proposed plan might disincline youth from marriage and spread moral disintegration and familial fragmentation." The League declared that the intention to raise the marriage

age, facilitate divorce, and limit polygamy was "incompatible with the laws of Allah" and "a deviation from the *Shari'a*."[16] Nadia Yacine, a leading female Moroccan Islamist, has also voiced dissatisfaction with the plan. In a 12 March 2000 interview, she asserted:

> This plan is an aggression against our religion and our culture. It is a tool fabricated for international organizations, for American imperialism. It is situated as an extension of the conferences of Nairobi, Delhi, and Beijing, that have been in favor of breaking the family cell, standing women against men, violating sacred values.[17]

Such religious opponents seek to slow the rate of change and strengthen religious influence within the government and society, replacing western notions of female equality with Islamist ideals of family values. They view any change in the *Mudawwana* as an affront on the *Shari'a*.[18] The fact, however, that a female Islamist even voiced her opinion publicly to a non-related male reporter, demonstrates that the situation for women in Morocco has changed from the days of harems and invisible women. As an active member of the Islamist community, Yacine, through her actions, as opposed to her words, ironically supports the nature of change within Morocco that has led to the modernization of the Code – the increasing participation of women in active Moroccan society through education, work, and public involvement.

Some women's liberation leaders and NGOs have complained that the changes to the Code of Personal Status do not go far enough and have not impacted the daily lives of all Moroccan women; religious groups believe the opposite. The changes, however, reflect the ideals that the cross-section of *'ulama* and political leaders who studied the issues, believe are most relevant to today's Moroccan woman. The shifts towards equality that this plan recommends therefore bolster the notion that women have become more active participants in the Moroccan political system, economy, and family since the creation of the Code of Personal Status at the time of independence. The next chapter examines the impact that the changes in the role of women in Morocco have had on life and relationships within the family.

NOTES

1. Bruce Maddy-Weitzman, "Women, Islam and the Moroccan State: The Struggle over the Personal Status Law," *Middle East Journal*, 59, No. 3 (Summer 2005), pp. 393–410.
2. ADFM, "Parallel Report of Moroccan NGOs"; Combe, p. 95.
3. ADFM, "Parallel Report of Moroccan NGOs."
4. Combe, p. 94.
5. 1992 Constitution of Morocco, Preamble.
6. ADFM, "Parallel Report of Moroccan NGOs."
7. "Reproductive Health in Policy and Practice: Case Studies from Brazil, India, Morocco, and Uganda" (Population Reference Bureau, 2005), <http://www.prb.org/>.
8. Sadiqi, p. 71; Aïcha El Hajjami, "La réforme de la condition juridique des femmes au Maroc; analyse d'un processus, Partie 2: Les Eneux du Débat sur le référentiel," (Centre d'Etudes Internationales, 2005), <www.centreinter.com>.
9. El Hajjami, Partie 1.
10. There are 325 total seats.
11. US Department of State, "Morocco," *Country Reports on Human Rights Practices*, February 28, 2005, Section 3, <http://www.state.gov/g/drl/rls/hrrpt/2004/41728.htm>.
12. Carol Anne Douglas and Palmer Gibbs, "Morocco: new family code is both progressive and backward," *Off Our Backs*, 34, Issue 9/10 (Sep/Oct 2004), p. 5.
13. Soumaya Belhabib, "Moroccan Women's NGOs: Civil Society's Agents of Change." Proceedings of the Third AIWF Annual Conference: Women in the Arab World Partners in the Community and on the World Stage, 6–9 June 2004 (Cairo, Egypt: League of Arab States Headquarters, 2004), p. 4.; El Hajjami, Partie 1.
14. Population Reference Bureau.
15. El Hajjami, Partie 4.
16. *Al-Hayāt, "Rābita 'Ulamā' al-Maghrib Tuntaqadu 'Idmāj al-Mar'a fī al-Tanmiya',"* 21 June 1999.
17. Marc Yared, "Nadia Yacine: 'Nous Irons Aux, Elections Si…'," *Arabies* (February 2001), pp. 20–25.
18. El Hajjami, Partie 4.

Chapter 10

On Family Life and Gender Relations

While alterations in the Code of Personal Status may propel further change in the status of women, they were also designed to reflect a new situation in Morocco – one in which many women were already more empowered than the laws allowed. The empowerment of women at home and in male/female relations in general, has resulted from changes in the role of women in society. In return, innovations in family structure enable women to become more active outside of the house. The effect, then, is one of mutual reinforcement. Such change in the family and social framework also creates dissonance, as people are pulled between tradition and innovation. Changes are far from uniform throughout Moroccan households, and very few, if any, have impacted every aspect of society. This chapter looks at what these changes outside of the house mean for women workers at home, how relationships between men and women have been affected by workforce participation, and the impact of female labor force participation on the institution of marriage.

Education, Employment, and Familial Relations Among Women

Working outside of the house can impact a woman's familial relations in different ways, depending on her initial role in the family, the nature of her work, and the attitudes of family members. For some educated young brides, their knowledge and jobs increase their standing within the hierarchy of women in the household. Instead of turning to their mothers-in-law to learn about cooking or childcare, educated women can read recipes and books about child development for themselves. In these cases, dependency has been reversed, causing the older generation to rely on the younger one for assistance with court representation, taking prescription drugs, and other basic tasks required to function in modern, urban society. Earning an income to help support the family gives educated women greater power, too, since they have "more or less bought their clout."[1] For some, this hierarchy no longer exists. As people move to urban areas, smaller, more intimate families, in which women may not even need to seek the approval of their mothers-in-law for household power, have replaced the extended clan. With this change, however, some working women have faced added domestic burdens.

Many women must continue to meet all of their familial and household responsibilities in addition to their labors outside of the house. With increasing labor migration, the extended nuclear family, which in the past formed a woman's support network, may no longer be available for a woman to rely upon.[2] Some working women can afford to hire maids or domestic helpers to assist with the childcare and household chores that the women of the more extended family used to complete together. This results in a boost for the female service economy. In response, more and more women have begun to market themselves as maids.[3] Not all working women, however, are so lucky as to be in a position to hire help for their domestic duties. Some families simply cannot afford it, even with the wife's salary. In other households, the daughter, not the wife, is the one who works.

An unmarried daughter has much less household clout than her mother, and for her, working does not equal empowerment or independence. In some families, earning income through factory work is viewed as one of a daughter's many duties. A young factory employee must still help her mother with household chores, childcare, and other duties around the house.[4] In many households in which family members work in low-paying factories, every eligible family member works. A study by Laetitia Cairoli informs that 89% of workers interviewed reported contributing some or all of their salaries to the family.[5] The fact that a factory worker's wages are so low and the work so unstable that it does not allow a woman to fully support herself, let alone her family, leaves her position in the household unchanged. Women in factories are thus at the mercy of their parents' wishes at home and their bosses' demands at work. The nature of the job and lack of education required means that it rarely brings the worker prestige or additional power in familial or societal relations.

Regardless of all of these negatives, however, many young women see factory employment as "emancipatory" in certain ways. It allows them to escape familial authority, at least during work hours. Daughters do not always keep their families abreast of every nuance in factory scheduling. Rahma Bourqia describes how some young women take advantage of this position:

> Some factories, when they have no orders, give one or two days' leave to the women workers while waiting for new orders. When this happens, some women leave home for the factory, pretending to their parents that they are going to do a day's work there. But instead, they spend the day walking about the streets in town.[6]

With all of its hardships and potential negatives, therefore, the fact that factory work enables a woman to escape the confines of her home and direct eye of her parents allows her a certain degree of personal liberty, even without substantial financial independence.

Women in Male Spaces

As women go to work and the traditional relationship between a man and a woman shifts, some men feel threatened. Fatima Mernissi explains this change in terms of female trespass on male space:

> When women go to work they are not only trespassing in the universe of the *umma* but are also competing with their former masters, men, for the scarce available jobs. The anxiety created by women seeking jobs in the modern sector, and thus demanding a role traditionally reserved for men, inevitably aggravates tension and conflict because of the scarcity of jobs and the high state of unemployment among men.[7]

Male honor is further endangered as the spatial barrier between male and female spaces breaks down. A man's prestige hinges in no small part on the behavior of his wife and female kin. As women enter public spaces at school and work, there is a greater chance that they may do something to offend family honor. "To have men's honour embodied in women's sexual behaviour was a much safer system when women's space was strictly confined to the courtyard and ritual visits to the *hammam* or the local saint's tomb."[8] This separation, however, is no longer feasible as women work to help their families survive or to maintain their desired lifestyle.

Women who enter "male spaces" through education and work are often harassed. At work, a man may get "confused" with the role of a secretary subordinate to him, and treat her diminutively or make sexual advances.[9] In some areas, especially public sector employment, women have avenues of complaint, and such behavior is condemned. In informal or unsupervised formal employment, however, subordinate female employees may be physically or sexually harassed, and even raped. It is socially acceptable in Morocco, for example, to beat maids.[10] Some women have begun to fight back against such invasion and aggravation. They have gained support from feminist and human rights groups, who help them organize and protest sexual harassment in the workplace.[11] A lack of familial support for a woman's role outside of the house and a dearth of respect in the office environment make working a potentially trying undertaking for women, emotionally and physically.

Women, Work, and Marriage Relations

Education and employment have altered the nature of marriage and finding a marriage partner for many Moroccan men and women. While certain customs have remained the same, brides have not. Thus, Deborah Kapchan explains, "the bride may still be considered a gift between families, but her packaging has considerably changed."[12] A woman's new "packaging" may impact her search for a marriage partner, her relationship with her husband, and the potential for her marriage to end in divorce.

It can be difficult for educated women to find a husband, especially one with whom they are satisfied. Many men do not want a wife that will question what they do. A female student at a training college who had many male friends that valued being able to talk with an educated woman but would never dream of marrying one explains why: "They want someone who will be content to sit at home and be their servant. They don't want any contestation."[13] The situation was similar in the small Moroccan town of Zawiya, in which Douglas Davis researched Moroccan relationships. There, he found that even those adolescents who intended to combine career and family and share two incomes actually ended up marrying younger, less educated girls who would defer to them and their families. Those that did marry someone of equivalent age and education to themselves usually selected a spouse from school or work in another city. Some educated local girls, therefore, had not married, and others only did so after going to a larger city and meeting someone with similar education.[14]

Education and employment also impact the nature of a woman's relationship with her husband. Jobs and education enable many women to be more assertive in their marriages. "Once women have their own source of income, their influence in the household changes from covert to overt and they feel much more confident of their own control and especially their security."[15] Even with more security, however, women must still meet their wifely responsibilities. Many men who enjoy the fact that their wives bring home paychecks refuse to help out around the house. Kapchan describes her friend Fadela, whose home life reflects such a situation:

> She works fulltime while also performing all the responsibilities of a Moroccan housewife. She prepares breakfast and lunch before leaving for work in the morning, walks half a mile uphill to her office, returns home for lunch, serves and cleans up, returns again to work, comes home and prepares dinner. Her husband brings the children to and from school, but does not cook, clean, wash, or do any other traditionally female tasks.[16]

Thus with added freedom and rights within the household come more responsibility. Not only do urban working women lack the extended familial safety net, but they also take on more "male" responsibilities of helping to support the family, while their husbands refuse to assist with "women's work." In many instances in which women are educated, their husbands still have a better education or job. As such, women wage earners tend to earn less than their husbands and believe that their husbands' promotions are more important than their own. This is even the case if the husband and wife hold the same position at the same company.[17] Such sentiments demonstrate that the patriarchal societal foundations of Moroccan society remain, even if women have begun to exercise more liberties beyond the boundaries of the house.

Divorce may result when a wife's independence or income creates conflict at home. The nature of Islamic law on the matter sometimes leads to such discord. According to Islamic law, the husband is the sole provider for the family, and a woman's income and property remain her own. Quarrels result when the husband expects his wife to turn over all of her income to the benefit of the household when he fails to do the same. Ziba Mir-Hosseini recounts a case in which such arguments ended a marriage:

> Nadia and Ahmad had dated in university and even lived together for a year before marriage. However, when they got married, Nadia resented the fact that part of Ahmad's salary went to his siblings, and Ahmad had

a separate social life and wouldn't help out at home. In response, Nadia refused to spend her income from a private sector job in the house. She explained 'Why should I invest whatever I have, my youth and my money, in our marriage so that his family benefits?' They divorced after nine months.[18]

For Nadia, Ahmad's double standard was unacceptable. She had the power to divorce him because her income enabled her to support herself. Such personal and financial independence is necessary for a woman to truly fight for the rights that she believes she deserves.

Many families have the wives remain at home while sending their unmarried daughters to work, in order to avoid the situation in which a wife's salary undermines her husband's control of the household. Of the factory women, Cairoli surveyed, 76% had never been married.[19] While Islamic Family Law guarantees wives economic protection in marriage and the right to keep any wages they earn, daughters do not enjoy such privilege and must turn over their earnings to their families. It is also more socially acceptable for young, single women to work since "it is seen as a temporary situation until they marry or until the family's fortunes improve."[20] Factory owners, too, prefer to hire single women because they are easier to exploit. Husbands would be shamed and outraged if married women were forced to work long hours under sometimes demeaning conditions and could not perform their duties at home.[21]

As this chapter demonstrates, there are a variety of responses within and among families to the entrance of women into the workforce. A woman's ability to stand up for and support herself within the family and at work depends on her level of education and income as well as her position in the family. Many families in Morocco are still negotiating, therefore, over what they view as proper female behavior and appropriate gender relations in households in which women work. The higher the education and income level of a woman, the more say she has in what her role in the household should be. Regardless, however, certain areas of responsibility remain under a wife's domain. Most husbands refuse to help out with "womanly" tasks around the house. As such, women must serve double duty at home and on the job, or hire maids instead.

NOTES

1. Kapchan, pp. 213–215.
2. Naila Minai, *Women in Islam: Tradition and Transition in the Middle East* (London: John Murray, 1981), p. 215.
3. Kapchan, p. 220.
4. Bourqia, p. 40.
5. Cairoli, p. 37.
6. Bourqia, p. 71.
7. Mernissi, *Beyond the Veil*, p. 146.
8. *Ibid*, p. 161.
9. *Ibid*, p. 146.
10. Kapchan, p. 232.
11. Moghadam, *Women, Work and Economic Reform*, p. 73.
12. Kapchan, p. 153.
13. Maher, p. 88.
14. Douglas A. Davis, "Modernizing the Sexes: Changing Gender Relations in a Moroccan Town," in A. Schlegel (ed.), *Special Issue on Adolescence, Ethos* (1995), 23, pp. 69–78.
15. Susan S. Davis, p. 71.
16. Kapchan, p. 155.
17. Sadiqi, p. 72.
18. Mir-Hosseini, pp. 122, 123.
19. Cairoli, p. 37
20. Bourqia, p. 71.
21. Cairoli, pp. 42–43.

Chapter 11

On Demographics and Family Planning

The changes in the structure of the Moroccan family and societal expectations of women, in conjunction with specific government policies, have impacted family planning in Morocco. According to Jennifer Olmstead, the rise in female labor force participation has led to a decline in fertility rates since women are the main childcare providers in the family: "Increased wage-based employment opportunities, by pulling women into the labor market, have thus contributed to reducing fertility rates."[1] This corresponds with Karshenas's hypothesis that the number of children per mother decreases and more women enter the labor force as the earning power of women rises and women can earn more in the wage-based labor market than they can save on childcare by staying at home and caring for children. This chapter examines these hypotheses by comparing differences between Morocco's family planning experience and Egypt's as a result of differentials in the economic climates, workforce participation rates, and marriage ages of the two countries.

Fertility Rates and Family Planning Campaigns in Egypt and Morocco

In the 1960s, both Egypt and Morocco initiated family planning programs, at a time when fertility rates stood approximately at seven children per woman (see Table 1). As Table 1 demonstrates, Egypt's program began more forcefully, and the country initially experienced a quick drop in fertility to 5.5 births per woman by 1972. The Moroccan government began its first attempts at family planning in February 1966. This plan, however, occurred without such necessary preparations as making contraceptive devices available, addressing the status of women, liberalizing abortion laws, or providing doctors with funding to

---

implement the program.[2] As a result, the initial years of the Moroccan program met with little success. Fertility rates only decreased by 0.3% between 1960 and 1972 to 6.9 births per woman in 1972. Then, from 1972 to 2002, fertility rates declined much more rapidly in Morocco (60.1%) than in Egypt (41.8%). By 1982, Morocco had a birthrate equivalent to that in Egypt, with 5.1 births per woman, and by 2002, Morocco had clearly surpassed Egypt with a birthrate of 2.75 births per woman, as opposed to Egypt's 3.2. At the start of the fertility program, most experts agreed that Egypt was in a better position to succeed than Morocco. What, then, accounts for the quicker drop in Moroccan fertility rates after the mid-1970s?

Table 1: Fertility Rate, Total (Births per Woman)

Country	1960	1965	1970	1972	1975	1980	1982	1985	1990	1992	1995	2002
Egypt	7.0	6.8	6.0	5.5	5.4	5.1	5.1	4.6	4.0	3.8	3.6	3.2
Morocco	7.2	7.1	7.0	6.9	6.3	5.4	5.1	4.7	4.0	3.8	3.4	2.75

Source: World Bank, DevData

Fertility Rates and the Economy

In Egypt, more rapid economic growth since the mid-1970s did not lead to a substantial decrease in fertility; in Morocco, slow economic growth did. One of the main causes for this difference was the household economic situation. A slow economy in the late 1970s and early 1980s forced Moroccan households to conserve their resources and led to the need for two-income families. This is especially evident during the years in which Morocco lost much of its income from phosphate rents. Table 1 demonstrates that between 1972 and 1980, the Moroccan fertility rate decreased from 6.9 to 5.4. Egypt benefited from the oil wealth of nearby MENA countries, and the average household did not face the same fiscal strain as that in Morocco. Thus, families in Egypt did not change their demographic patterns as quickly.[3]

As Table 2 demonstrates, between 1970 and 1990, as Morocco's birthrate decreased at rates much faster than Egypt's, Morocco's female labor force participation rate increased. By 1990, Morocco's female labor force participation rate was 34.5%, 7.4% higher than that in Egypt. In addition to the higher rate of labor force participation in Morocco, according to Youssef

Courbage, "Wage work is associated with a 50 percent decline in fertility in Morocco, but only a 37 percent decline in Egypt."[4] Thus, not only were more women employed in Morocco, but employment had a greater impact on fertility rates in Morocco than in Egypt. Since 1990, Egypt has narrowed the female labor force participation gap between it and Morocco, but Morocco's participation rates continue to edge up as its birthrate declines.

Table 2: Labor Force % Female

	1965	1970	1975	1980	1985	1990	1995	2000	2004
Morocco (% Female)	29.9	31.4	32.6	33.5	34.0	34.5	34.6	34.7	35.3
Egypt (% Female)	25.1	25.9	26.2	26.5	26.8	27.1	28.9	30.5	31.7
Difference		4.8	5.5	6.4	7.0	7.2	7.4	5.7	4.2	3.6

Source: World Bank, DevData

Marriage Age, Fertility Rates, and Workforce Participation

Workforce participation in Morocco is also related to a higher marriage age than in Egypt. In 1960, the average marriage age in Morocco was 17. In Egypt, it was 20. By 1992, the average marriage age in Morocco had risen to 25, but it plateaued at 22 in Egypt in 1988.[5] This sharp increase of eight years in the Moroccan marriage age between 1960 and 1992 can be at least partially accounted for by the increase in female labor force participation. Women in the workforce do not necessarily have to depend on men for support, so they can defer marriage to a later age. In addition, an early dearth of money and the necessity to work are factors that postpone marriage, especially as extended family networks decline, and men and women must earn money to support their families before marriage is feasible.

The later women marry, the fewer children they tend to have. R. Assaad and S. Zuoari confirmed this relationship between marriage age, children, and workforce participation through a survey of 3,323 urban Moroccan households in 1991. They spoke with women aged 15 through 54 and determined that women in the active labor force tended to marry at a later age and have fewer children than non-wage workers and non-labor force participants (see Table 3). Those in public sector jobs, which generally require the most education, have the latest marriage age and lowest total number of children. Private wage workers, who may work in more informal occupations and have lower education levels, marry slightly younger, at 19, and average slightly more children. Those who are inactive or work for no wages average the lowest marriage ages, at 18.36 and 17.35 respectively, and the highest number of children, at 4.06 and 3.92.

Table 3: Work Status, Marriage Age, and Children

WORK STATUS	INACTIVE	NON-WAGE WORKER	UNEMPLOYED	PRIVATE WAGE WORKER	PUBLIC WAGE WORKER
Age at Marriage	18.26	17.35	18.43	19.08	21.15
Total # of Children	4.06	3.92	2.42	2.69	2.24

Source: Assaad and Zouari from the Moroccan Living Standards Measurement Study

As women choose or are forced to earn more money for their families and can do so best by working outside of the house, fertility rates decline. This occurs since having additional children means more time a woman cannot be at work, added expenses, and higher childcare costs, especially as extended family networks disintegrate with rural to urban migration. When women toil at home in unofficial labor sectors, they can more readily care for their children while concurrently working informally. This is not the case in a factory. Therefore, the combination of a higher Moroccan marriage age, disintegration of extended family structures, prevalence of manufacturing jobs, and the need to work best explain the differences in the results of the Moroccan and Egyptian family planning programs.

NOTES

1. Olmsted, p. 75.
2. Bruce Maddy-Weitzman, "Population Growth and Family Planning in Morocco," *Asian and African Studies*, 26, No. 1 (March 1992), pp. 68, 69.
3. Courbage, p. 21.
4. *Ibid.*
5. *Ibid*, p. 20.

Conclusion

Throughout the second half of the twentieth century, despite religious and social mores seemingly to the contrary, increasing numbers of women began to work for wages in Morocco. Although some women in prior decades and centuries had worked for money, these women were usually socially stigmatized because they did not have a male caretaker and thus were forced to interact with strangers in public to survive. Such norms did not suddenly disappear with the increase in Moroccan women in the labor force and have been partially responsible for the nature of work in which women engage. In recent years, however, these ideals have shifted as women have become more active members of Moroccan society.

Since women in Morocco hail from a plethora of backgrounds and social strata, the growth in female participation in the Moroccan labor force following the end of French colonial rule in 1956 resulted from a number of factors. From the late 1800s through the end of Moroccan colonialism, slowly increasing numbers of Moroccan women gained an education. As women's liberation accompanied the nationalist movement towards the end of the 1940s and 1950s, calls for women's literacy and education increased. Since independence, various government-run literacy campaigns have slowly raised literacy rates among men and women, providing women with the tools to better compete for jobs and actively participate in society. Urbanization, initiated during the colonial period, increased in post-colonial times as European companies set up manufacturing shop in Morocco. Rural to urban migration ensued as poorer rural and urban women moved to factory neighborhoods to work in the manufacturing sector. When the phosphate crisis of the 1970s hit Morocco, and the economic condition of Moroccan households deteriorated throughout the late 1970s and 1980s, women began to work in greater numbers to maintain their families' standards of living, or just to make ends meet. The manufacturing sector grew, and the number of women in public sector employment, the skilled workforce, and informal labor increased as well. Thus, the increase in women in the labor force since 1970 occurred because of increased educational opportunities for women, financial hardship and need, rural to urban migration, and changes in prevailing social stigmas against working women and their male relatives who permitted them to work.

Change, however, comes slow, and many opponents to female participation in public spheres remain. In this regard, efforts by NGOs, women's organizations, the Moroccan government, and especially Kings Hassan II and Muhammad VI have been key instigators of societal change regarding women and their role in Moroccan society. King Muhammad VI built upon the basis for change that his father, Hassan the II had initiated, culminating in recent far-reaching alterations of the *Mudawwana*. These changes, which occurred after decades of struggle on the part of women's organizations, lay a new foundation for the rights of women in Moroccan society. Devised at the behest of King Muhammad VI by a committee that sought to adjust the Code to the modern realities for Moroccan women, the fact that women are now treated as nearly full, equal citizens under Moroccan law says a great deal about the active role that women play in Moroccan society today, at least in the eyes of the government.

Integral building blocks for the foundation for change were placed in the 1980s, as Morocco became increasingly beholden to international institutions such as the World Bank and IMF for its financial stability. As Morocco has remained dependent on international organizations, the government has kept an ear tuned to the priorities expressed by these bodies and their key member states. Thus, the international emphasis on women and human rights influenced the Moroccan government and specifically, its policy towards women. International treaties have impacted Morocco's legal and political debate about women and human rights, leading to the addition of the human rights clause to Morocco's 1992 Constitution. Creating a legal basis for equality, however, is merely the first step towards actually realizing it. Laws must be enforced and social views shifted in order for the spirit of the changes to apply to Moroccan women in their daily lives.

The entrance of women into the Moroccan workforce since 1970 also caused change and new stresses to occur, beyond the realm of legislation, in Moroccan family life. Wives who earn incomes have tested the fabrics of some Moroccan families, as they struggle to devise acceptable ways to distribute household income and responsibilities. Social norms have not shifted to the point that Moroccan men are generally willing to assist with traditionally female household responsibilities. As a result, jobs outside of the house usually mean double the work for Moroccan women. As the extended family structure has dissipated with urbanization, and women do more work outside of the house, the marriage age has increased, and the number of children per mother has gone down.

The financial liberty that a job provides can empower a wife to assert herself more than she could in the past. In many two-income households in which both the wife and husband work, the wife is regarded more highly among other women in the family, as well as in relations with her husband. In other households, however, male members have had trouble relinquishing their role as the sole money earner and unquestioned decision-maker; as a result some marriages have disintegrated, and some educated women have had trouble finding a partner.

Some working women, moreover, are arguably worse off because of their entrance into the workforce. Poor, unskilled, uneducated women, who participate in informal employment, often fall below the radar of law enforcement officials. These women are often employed as maids, vendors, or in unregulated factories, and are subject to exploitation. They may be forced to work long hours, denied overtime pay or benefits, harassed physically or sexually, and stigmatized by society. The opportunities of the labor force allow these women to eke out a living, but this comes at great personal expense. Gender discrimination against women workers relegates women to such undesirable positions, and societal prejudices against undesirable women reinforce their place at the bottom of the social ladder.

There are a number of social and religious factors for women to contend with in the pursuit of self-sufficiency. Allowing women to work, however, is a start towards more gender equality in Morocco. Women are already gaining more control of their lives through family planning and new legislation. The entrance of women into the Moroccan labor force during the final decades of the twentieth century laid the foundations for these changes that the Moroccan legislature voted into effect in 2004. To further the situation of women workers in Morocco, the government must enforce its laws governing the treatment of workers and female equality. It is therefore up to Morocco's legislators and law enforcement leaders to determine the course of women's rights in unskilled, low-paid sectors, and it is up to Moroccan parents to educate both their male and female children to provide them with equal tools to steer the courses of their own futures. As the preceding decades demonstrated, only as women gain education and become vocal, labor force participants, are their voices for change heard, and their rights as equal citizens granted.

Works Cited

Agnaou, Fatima. *Gender, Literacy, and Empowerment in Morocco*. New York: Routledge, 2004.

Amin, Qasim. *The Liberation of Women*. Translated by Samiha Sidhom Peterson. Cairo, Egypt: American University of Cairo Press, 1992.

Assaad, R. and S. Zouari. "Estimating the Impact of Marriage and Fertility on the Female Labor Force Participation when Decisions are Interrelated: Evidence from Urban Morocco," in E. M. Cinar (ed.), *Topics in Middle Eastern and North African Economies*, Vol. 5. Middle East Economic Association and Loyola University Chicago, September, 2003. <http://www.luc.edu/publications/academic/>.

Association Démocratique des Femmes du Maroc. "Parallel Report of Moroccan NGOs on the Application of the Convention on Eliminating all forms of Discrimination Against Women (CEDAW)." Rabat, Morocco. December 1996. [ADFM, "Parallel Report of Moroccan NGOs"].

Belghazi, Saâd and Sally Baden. "Wage discrimination by gender in Morocco's urban labour force: Evidence and implications for industrial and labour policy," in Carol Miller and Jessica Vivian (eds.), *Women's Employment in the Textile Manufacturing Sectors of Bangladesh and Morocco*. Geneva, Switzerland: UNRISD and UNDP, 2002, pp. 35–60.

Belhabib, Soumaya. "Moroccan Women's NGOs: Civil Society's Agents of Change." *Proceedings of the Third AIWF Annual Conference: Women in the Arab World Partners in the Community and on the World Stage, 6–9 June 2004*. Cairo, Egypt: League of Arab States Headquarters, 2004.

Bourqia, Rahma. "Gender and Employment in Moroccan Textile Industries," in Carol Miller and Jessica Vivian (eds.), *Women's Employment in the Textile Manufacturing Sectors of Bangladesh and Morocco*. Geneva, Switzerland: UNRISD and UNDP, 2002, pp. 61–102.

Cairoli, M. Laetitia. "Garment Factory Workers in the City of Fez," *The Middle East Journal*, Vol. 53, No. 1 (Winter 1999), pp. 28–43.

Charrad, Mounira M. *States and Women's Rights: The Making of Postcolonial Tunisia, Algeria, and Morocco*. Berkeley: University of California Press, 2001.

Clinton, Hillary Rodham, et al. "Moroccan Women's Roundtable Discussion with the First Lady." Marrakech, Morocco, 30 March 1999. Retrieved April 2005. <http://www.usinfo.state.gov/usa/womenusa/hilround.htm>.

Combe, Julie. *La Condition de la Femme Marocaine.* Paris: L'Harmattan, 2001.

Combs-Schilling, Elaine. "Performing Monarchy, Staging Nation," in Rahma Bourqia and Susan Gilson Miller (eds.), *In the Shadow of the Sultan: Culture, Power, and Politics in Morocco.* Cambridge, MA: Harvard University Press, 1999, pp. 176–214.

Courbage, Youssef. "Demographic Change in the Arab World: The Impact of Migration, Education and Taxes in Egypt and Morocco," *Middle East Report,* No. 190 (September–October 1994), pp. 19–22.

Daoud, Zakya. *Feminisme et Politique au Maghreb.* Casablanca: Editions Eddif, 1996.

Davis, Douglas A. "Modernizing the Sexes: Changing Gender Relations in a Moroccan Town," in A. Schlegel (ed.), *Special Issue on Adolescence, Ethos,* 1995, Vol. 23, pp. 69–78.

Davis, Susan S. *Patience and Power: Women's Lives in a Moroccan Village.* Cambridge, MA: Schenkman Publishing Company, 1983.

Denoeux, Guilain P. and Abdeslam Maghraoui. "The Political Economy of Structural Adjustment in Morocco," in Azzedine Layachi (ed.), *Economic Crisis and Political Change in North Africa.* Westport, CT: Praeger Publishers, 1998, pp. 55–89.

Douglas, Carol Anne and Palmer Gibbs. "Morocco: new family code is both progressive and backward," *Off Our Backs,* Vol. 34, Iss. 9/10 (Sep/Oct 2004), p. 5.

El Hajjami, Aïcha. "La réforme de la condition juridique des femmes au Maroc; analyse d'un processus." Centre d'Etudes Internationales, Partie 1-4. Retrieved January 19, 2005. <www.centreinter.com>.

El Mansour, Mohamad. "Moroccan Islam Observed," *The Maghreb Review,* Vol. 29, No. 1–4 (2004), pp. 208–218.

El Mikawy, Noha and Marsha Pripstein Posusney. "Labor Representation in the Age of Globalization: Trends and Issues in Non-Oil-Based Arab Economies," in Heba Handoussa and Zafiris Tzannatos (eds.), *Employment Creation and Social Protection in the Middle East and North Africa.* Cairo, Egypt: The American University of Cairo Press, 2002, pp. 49–94.

Entelis, John P. *Comparative Politics of North Africa: Algeria, Morocco, and Tunisia.* Syracuse, New York: Syracuse University Press, 1980.

Fernea, Elizabeth Warnock. *A Street in Marrakech.* Prospect Heights, Il: Waveland Press, Inc., 1976.

Griffiths, Claire. "Social Development and Women in Africa: The Case of Morocco," *Journal of Gender Studies,* Vol. 5, Issue 1 (March 1996), pp. 63–79.

Al-Hayāt, "Rābita 'Ulamā' al-Maghrib Tuntaqadu 'Idmāj al-Mar'a fī al-Tanmiya'," 21 June 1999.

Hourani, Albert. *A History of the Arab Peoples.* New York: Warner Books, 1991.

International Labor Organization, Bureau of Statistics. *LABORSTA.* 1998–2004, retrieved in April 2005. < http://laborsta.ilo.org>.

International Women's Rights Action Watch. "Morocco." Retrieved 22 April 2005. <http://iwraw.igc.org/publications/countries/morocco.htm>. [IWRAW, "Morocco"].

Kandiyoti, Deniz. "Islam and Patriarchy: A Comparative Perspective," in Nikki R. Keddie and Beth Baron (eds.), *Women in Middle Eastern History: Shifting Boundaries in Sex and Gender.* New Haven, CT: Yale University Press, 1991.

Kapchan, Deborah. *Gender on the Market: Moroccan Women and the Revoicing of Tradition.* Philadelphia, PA: University of Pennsylvania Press, 1996.

Karshenas, Massoud. "Economic Liberalization, Competitiveness, and Women's Employment in the Middle East and North Africa," in Djavad Salehi-Isfahani (ed.), *Labor and Human Capital in the Middle East.* Reading, UK: Ithaca Press, 2001, pp. 147–194.

Kingdom of Morocco. *1992 Constitution.* Retrieved in April 2005. <http://www.oefre.unibe.ch/law/icl/mo00000_.html>.

Kozma, Liat. "Remembrance of Things Past: Leila Abouzeid and Moroccan National History," *Social Politics,* Vol. 6, Issue 3 (Fall 1999), pp. 388–406.

Lapidus, Ira M. *A History of Islamic Societies, Second Edition.* Cambridge, UK: Cambridge University Press, 2002.

Layachi, Azzedine. "State-Society Relations and Change in Morocco," in Azzedine Layachi (ed.), *Economic Crisis and Political Change in North Africa.* Westport, CT: Praeger Publishers, 1998, pp. 89–107.

Ligner, Isabelle. "Moroccan Women Fear Extremism," *Middle East Online – Women in Morocco,* [Casablanca], 22 May 2003. Retrieved in April 2005 <http://www.middle-east-online.com/english/?id=5670=5670&format=0>.

Maher, Vanessa. *Women and Property in Morocco: Their changing relation to the process of social stratification in the Middle Atlas.* London: Cambridge University Press, 1974.

Mao Zedong [Tse Tung]. *Quotations from Chairman Mao Tse Tung.* Beijing, China: Foreign Language Press, 1966.

Maddy-Weitzman, Bruce. "Population Growth and Family Planning in Morocco," *Asian and African Studies,* Vol. 26, No. 1 (March 1992), pp. 63–79.

_____. "Women, Islam and the Moroccan State: The Struggle over the Personal Status Law," *Middle East Journal,* Vol. 59, No. 3 (Summer 2005), pp. 393–410.

Mernissi, Fatima. *Beyond the Veil: Male-Female Dynamics in Modern Muslim Society, Revised Edition.* Indiana: Indiana University Press, 1987. [*Beyond the Veil*].

_____. *Dreams of Trespass: Tales of a Harem Girlhood*. Reading, Massachusetts: Addison-Wesley Publishing Company, Inc., 1994. [*Dreams of Trespass*].

Minai, Naila. *Women in Islam: Tradition and Transition in the Middle East*. London: John Murray, 1981.

Mir-Hosseini, Ziba. *Marriage on Trial: A Study of Islamic Family Law*. New York: I.B. Tauris and Co. Ltd., 1997.

Moghadam, Valentine. "Enhancing Women's Economic Participation in the MENA Region," in Heba Handoussa and Zafiris Tzannatos (eds.), *Employment Creation and Social Protection in the Middle East and North Africa*. Cairo, Egypt: The American University of Cairo Press, 2002, pp. 237–279.

_____. *Modernizing Women: Gender and Social Change in the Middle East*. Boulder, CO: Lynne Rienner Publishers, 1993. [*Modernizing Women*].

_____. *Women, Work and Economic Reform in the Middle East and North Africa*. Boulder, CO: Lynne Rienner Publishers, 1998. [*Women, Work and Economic Reform*].

NASA. *Continuity and Change in Her Work*. Retrieved March 2005 <http://quest.arc.nasa.gov/space/frontiers/activities/womanswork/chart.html>.

Olmsted, Jennifer. "Reexamining the Fertility Puzzle in MENA," in Eleanor Abdella Doumato and Marsha Pripstein Posusney (eds.), *Women and Globalization in the Arab Middle East: Gender, Economy and Society*. Boulder, CO: Lynne Rienner Publishers, 2003, pp. 73–95.

Pennell, C.R. *Morocco Since 1830: a History*. New York: New York University Press, 2000.

Pfeifer, Karen and Marsha Pripstein Posusney. "Arab Economies and Globalization: An Overview," in Eleanor Abdella Doumato and Marsha Pripstein Posusney (eds.), *Women and Globalization in the Arab Middle East: Gender, Economy and Society*. Boulder, CO: Lynne Rienner Publishers, 2003, pp. 25–55.

Population Reference Bureau. *Reproductive Health in Policy and Practice: Case Studies from Brazil, India, Morocco, and Uganda*. Retrieved April 2005. <http://www.prb. org/>.

"Professional Training Centres for Young Women in Morocco." The Xinhua General Overseas News Service, 8 March 1979.

Rausch, Margaret. *Bodies, Boundaries and Spirit Possession: Moroccan Women and the Revision of Tradition*. New Brunswick, NJ: Transaction Publishers, 2000.

Rhazaoui, Ahmed. "Recent Economic Trends: Managing the Indebtedness," in I. William Zartman (ed.), *The Political Economy of Morocco*. New York: Praeger, 1987, pp. 141–158.

Rosen, Lawrence. *Bargaining for Reality: The Construction of Social Relations in a Muslim Community*. Chicago: University of Chicago Press, 1984.

Sabagh, Georges. "The Challenges of Population Growth in Morocco," *Middle East Report,* No. 181 (March–April, 1993), pp. 30–35.

Sadiqi, Fatima. "The Language of Women in the City of Fès, Morocco," *International Journal of the Sociology of Language,* Vol. 112. New York: Mouton de Gruyter, 1995, pp. 63–79.

Sorensen, Ninna Nyberg. "Migrant Remittances as a Development Tool: The Case of Morocco," *Migration Policy Research*, No. 2 (June 2004), pp. 1–16.

Swearingen, Will D. *Moroccan Mirages: Agrarian Dreams and Deceptions, 1912–1986*. London: I.B. Taurus & Co. Ltd., 1988.

Tzannatos, Zafiris and Iqbal Kaur. "Women in the MENA Labor Market: An Eclectic Survey," in Eleanor Abdella Doumato and Marsha Pripstein Posusney (eds.), *Women and Globalization in the Arab Middle East: Gender, Economy and Society*. Boulder, CO: Lynne Rienner Publishers, 2003, pp. 55–73.

United Nations. UNSTATS. United Nations Statistical Database. Retrieved 29 July 2005. <http://unstats.un.org/unsd>.

U.S. Department of State, Bureau of Democracy, Human Rights, and Labor, "Morocco," *Country Reports on Human Rights Practices*, 1999–2005. Retrieved January 13, 2006. <http://www.state.gov/g/drl/rls/hrrpt/2004/41728.htm>.

Waltz, Susan E. *Human Rights and Reform: Changing the Face of North African Politics*. Berkeley, CA: University of California Press, 1995.

World Bank. *Gender and Development in the Middle East and North Africa: Women and the Public Sphere: Overview.* Retrieved April 2004. <http://lnweb18.worldbank.org/mna/mena.nsf/Sectors/MNSED/477357DEBA73285B85256DEF0076D1CF? OpenDocument>.

_____. *World Development Indicators Database.* Retrieved April 2005. <http://devdata. worldbank.org/dataonline>.

_____. *Global Finance Development,* No. 2, 2005.

Yared, Marc. "Nadia Yacine: 'Nous Irons Aux, Elections Si…'," *Arabies*, February 2001, pp. 20–25.

Xinhua General Overseas News Service, "Professional Training Centres for Young Women in Morocco," 8 March 1979.

Additional Works Referenced

Davis, Douglas A. and Susan Schaefer Davis. "Possessed by Love: Gender and Romance in Morocco," in W. Jankowiak (ed.), *Romantic Passion: A universal experience?* New York: Columbia University Press, 1995, pp. 219–238.

"Education, marriages Tardifs, contraception, mentalités: Les Marocains veulent moins d'enfants," *L'Economiste* [Casablanca], 16 Feb. 1995: Economie.

Eltigani, Elgitani E. "Changes in Family-Building Patterns in Egypt and Morocco: A Comparative Analysis," *International Family Planning Perspectives*, Vol. 26, Issue 2 (June 2000).

Growing Faster, Finding Jobs: Choices for Morocco. Washington, D.C.: The World Bank, 1996.

Posusney, Marsha Pripstein and Eleanor Abdella Doumato. "Introduction: The Mixed Blessing of Globalization," in Eleanor Abdella Doumato and Marsha Pripstein Posusney (eds.), *Women and Globalization in the Arab Middle East: Gender, Economy and Society.* Boulder, CO: Lynne Rienner Publishers, 2003, pp. 1–25.

"Reports from Around the World: Middle East and Africa; Morocco; Women Demand Change," *Lexington*, Vol. 28, Issue. 4 (Autumn 2002), p. 60.

Sebti, Fadéla. *Life as a Muslim Woman in Morocco.* Translation from the Book Version, originally written in French, 1999. Retrieved 19 April 2005. <www.techno.net.ma/femmes/e-vivre.htm>.

Zartman, I. William (ed.). *The Political Economy of Morocco.* New York: Praeger, 1987.